The WILMINGTON, BRUNSWICK & SOUTHERN RAILROAD

The WILMINGTON, BRUNSWICK & SOUTHERN RAILROAD

Mark W. Koenig

The History Press

Published by The History Press
Charleston, SC
www.historypress.com

Front cover, top: Southport Train Station; *bottom*: WB&S Locomotive 101.
Back cover, top: Plymouth industrial locomotive; *bottom*: railroad map, 1917.

First published 2022

Manufactured in the United States

ISBN 9781467150378

Library of Congress Control Number: 2021949223

CONTENTS

ACKNOWLEDGEMENTS

Grateful acknowledgement for support and assistance is given to:

The Wilmington Railroad Museum, where the story of railroad history and heritage is told, with special emphasis on the Atlantic Coast Line Railroad; where a library of 1,100 volumes amply portrays the influential sweep of the railroad industry on settlement and economic growth, technical development and cultural currents; where I found opportunities to present and illustrate elements of the railroad story with a dedicated board of trustees.

Charles Kernan, whose book *Rails to Weeds: Searching Out the Ghost Railroads Around Wilmington* triggered curiosity about where the tracks ran, along with surface references and images.

The Southport Historical Society, where a speaking engagement about the Wilmington, Brunswick & Southern Railroad sparked a research effort of several years to delve into the life and times of this almost forgotten line through the interior of Brunswick County. The carefully organized resources of the Susie Carson Research Room provided consequential insights about Southport history and the context for the coming of the railroad.

The *State Port Pilot*. Thanks to Morgan Harper for graciously allowing the perusal of bound volumes, especially for the frequent images and captions contained in "The Way It Was" historical series.

To readers Marilyn Raschka, JimKapetsky and Bob Surridge, for constructive observations about the narrative, additional insights, fine-tuning details and contextual information.

Acknowledgements

To my wife, Calverna, whose keen eyes picked out compositional goofs, whose patient forbearance allowed the spread of materials on various tables around the house and whose good-natured tolerance permitted me to "get lost" to explore physical locations or to wander among the narrative byways of this work.

INTRODUCTION

This book had a long gestation. Over the course of my twelve-year tenure at the Wilmington Railroad Museum in North Carolina, I learned bits and pieces of information about the Wilmington, Brunswick & Southern Railroad (hereafter the WB&S), a short line that ran between Wilmington and Southport. Eventually, enough of those had accumulated to the point where some organization of the story seemed warranted.

There were apocryphal stories, some personal recollections, small news items from time to time, a few physical traces of its existence, assorted postcards and photographs—not necessarily in a jumble but certainly not presented in the context of the life of an enterprise, either. Personal memories were also scanty; the railroad was basically gone by 1940, when the Southport Station met its explosive demise, like an emphatic exclamation point to the phrase "The end!"

And like any topic that gets explored at length, there were many side trails that led into the why's and how's of the railroad's formation and life. Here were found backgrounds of named characters, origins of place names, geographic revelations and interesting sidebar stories—even a murder! Incorporating larger and simultaneous events and trends posed a bit of a challenge (bank crises and railroad speculation, for instance, or highway building and railroad growth). However distant these events and trends were to the WB&S, they still exerted some influence on its formation and existence.

It can't be a seamless narrative; evidence of the road's existence can only be inferred by the few preserved items we have—grainy photographs, postcards, newspaper bits and the like. Diving deep into the weeds of the arcane and handwritten records of the county register of deeds office also provided insights about the company's pre-operating period. And as a registered corporation, there may be a paper trail of its existence in some dusty bureaucratic files; after all, it was nominally a stock corporation with reports and property records. Some bits could be uncovered in the arid narratives of annual reports from the North Carolina Corporation Commission, but the WB&S, by and large, operated well below notice.

So here we have a life-and-times story about a short-lived short line, similar in ways to so many others that came and went, but with its own peculiarities and nuances that should be remembered. There are high expectations, hollow promises, a dose of hubris and eventual resignation to the circumstances of reality. There is a lot to say, and I hope that the work proves useful.

WILLING BUT SLOW

A Common Tale

Every now and then people still mention the old Wilmington, Brunswick and Southern Railroad that was once a vital part of Southport. In fact, a whole book could be written about it!
—Bill Reaves, newspaper columnist and historical annotator, in "The Lake Counties: Yesterdays," circa 1974

In 1918, it is told, a few hundred soldiers stationed at Fort Caswell were eagerly looking forward to a liberty holiday up in Wilmington, a train trip of about two hours. In Southport, they clambered aboard the secondhand coaches pressed into service on the Wilmington, Brunswick & Southern Railroad (WB&S). Their spirits were undoubtedly high as they crowded on.

In due time, the conductor shouted his "All aboard!" and the old locomotive gave a couple of departure toots. Easing the throttle forward, the engineer was dismayed that his engine remained stalled on the tracks, unable to muster up the initial thrust to get the train moving. After a couple more attempts, a conference with the conductor yielded a novel solution.

Orders were passed to the soldiers to disembark and position themselves for a push assist. With probable good cheer, the soldiers stepped off the train and lined themselves up alongside the cars. At the signal to start, all pushed to get the train rolling and then jumped back aboard to continue their trip.

Soldiers from Fort Caswell on board the train at Southport, circa 1918. During this period, the fort, just a mile and a half away across open water, held about 1,500 troops. State Port Pilot, *"The Way It Was" series.*

This apocryphal tale—documentary evidence seems to be lacking altogether—is one of the anecdotes in the history of the WB&S, whose initials came to mean "Willing But Slow" in the course of its thirty-odd years as a rail link between Wilmington and Southport.

Chapter 1

SETTING THE STAGE

Between Wilmington and Southport in southeastern North Carolina, there are some tracts of land intended for development many years ago but never completed. Lying along the southern reaches of today's town of Boiling Spring Lakes, one finds sand streets that were cut through but never finished and unbuilt neighborhoods where tall pines now grow. In particular, along Ridge Road, a rutted and potholed sand thoroughfare, one is struck by its straight path two miles long. Infrequent creatures may put in an appearance, or a cluster of pitcher plants might be found alongside, or the breezes will sough through the trees, and there is an overall air of isolation.

Over one hundred years ago, the silence would have been broken twice a day by a locomotive chugging along that path. Here was the train of the Wilmington, Brunswick & Southern Railroad on its leisurely way between Southport and Wilmington, about thirty miles distant. It would likely have had a mixed consist, a passenger coach and a couple of freight cars, rolling along at a sedate fifteen to twenty miles per hour. On occasion, perhaps a small freight train would have made the trip between the morning and evening passenger runs.

The landscape in Brunswick County would have been much less settled than it is now. Back then, the county was populated by only fourteen thousand people distributed across one thousand square miles. Features of forest, swamp, river and tidal creeks would be as familiar then as they are today, except they would be far greater in extent. In short, there were a

Shown here is Ridge Road, south of Boiling Spring Lakes in Brunswick County, North Carolina. This two-mile tangent was one leg of the Wilmington, Brunswick & Southern Railroad (1907–43). *Photo by author, 2019.*

lot more spaces between places back then. Population was concentrated in a few towns (Southport, Bolivia, Supply, Shallotte, Lockwood Folly) near to navigable water or along the Wilmington-Georgetown Road, a holdover from the colonial era and the only major road in the county. Great swaths of the interior had not even been penetrated, much less settled.

With some exceptions, place names were in a fluid state. The sprinkling of settlements and towns might take the name of a landowner or principal figure, only to disappear or change as those reasons became obscure or obsolete. Connecting these places were informal roads, perhaps better called paths, that shifted, fell into disuse or were simply absorbed back to native condition as better substitutes would be planned and built.

A railroad ending at Southport seemed to be a good idea back then, and there were a surprising number of efforts to achieve that. Once the WB&S was established, however, several larger factors were in play that led to its demise. These included trends in the railroad industry that favored consolidation instead of start-ups; periodic financial distress in the economy, triggered by domestic underhandedness or upsets abroad; and emergence of improved roads and highways to supplant the position of the WB&S.

Chapter 2

BORN IN OPTIMISTIC SPECULATION

The idea of a rail route to Southport goes way back to the 1850s, when the town was known as Smithville. Coal and vast forests were being opened up and exploited in the North Carolina Piedmont, around the upper reaches of Deep River and farther west. Simply having those resources was one thing; how to get them to shipping points was quite another. Roads were impossible or sometimes impassable, waterways weren't navigable that far inland and the only railroad in the area ran entirely in the wrong direction.

For North Carolina, it was shown that if a railroad could be built to a southern port—in particular Wilmington or Smithville—transport would be much more efficient and faster than existing methods. This applied not only to the Deep River deposits, about forty-five miles northwest of Fayetteville, but potentially to areas deeper into the Piedmont and Appalachians. A shorter distance to port meant lower costs for the producers, and it would diversify the North Carolina economy, which depended heavily on agriculture.

The Civil War got in the way of those plans, and the rebuilding of existing railroads damaged during the conflict added a few more years to the delay. Nationally, the ambitious expansion of railroads, especially west of the Mississippi, was layered on top of rapidly rebuilt rail networks in the East. From the end of the Civil War to 1873, miles of track in the nation doubled from 30,000 to about 63,000. By 1890, that would swell again to about 175,000 miles.

The severe bank crisis and depression of 1873–79 greatly upset the railroad industry, its rampant speculation and labor relations. An "echo" recession

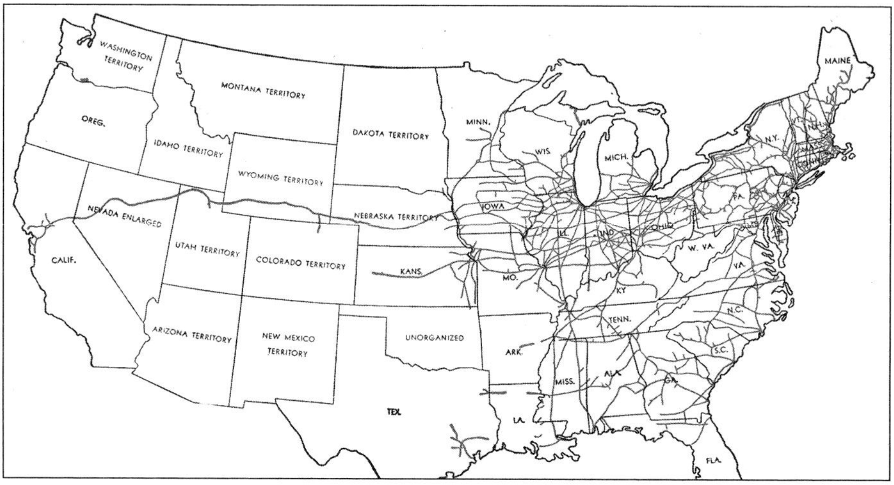

Comparison maps showing the great growth of railroads from 1870 (upper) to 1890 (lower). Note the relative absence of service where North Carolina, Tennessee, West Virginia and Virginia came together. This was the area where commodities needed an outlet to major shipping points. *railroad.net.*

of 1882–85 yielded some additional corrections, and railroads relaunched ambitious expansion efforts and were in the forefront of economic power. Having worked out standard gauges, standard time zones, reliable safety equipment (notably couplers and brakes), vastly improved rolling stock and greater applications of technology, they were a potent symbol of progress and importance. A booming steel industry provided rails and equipment components, and untapped forests yielded millions of crossties for construction.

Fueled by ready capital and a relatively unregulated environment, railroad magnates embarked on programs of mergers and acquisitions from the first wave of railroad expansion. Besides consolidating regional influence, they strengthened their competitive positions—with some dubious business practices—and railroad moguls were viewed by many as far too influential, combining high finance with low politics. (One example was Thomas Scott, president of the Pennsylvania Railroad and four others in the early 1870s. He was also vice president of another twelve railroads and director for thirty-three more.) With no real competition for overland travel, railroads exercised great control over the flow of freight and passengers.

The Thirteenth Census of the United States (1910) reported that out of about 24,600,000 people employed in non-agricultural labor, at least 1,500,000 were engaged in rail operations, freight and passenger operating service, station agents and communications. Another several hundred thousand would have been found in support roles for the railroad companies, including clerks and agents of all kinds in a bewildering array of seniority grades, ancillary station personnel, financial and auditing occupations, insurance, law, management at all levels, secretarial and stenographic personnel, real estate acquisition and management, engineering and architecture and manufacturing of machinery, rolling stock and equipment with its own collection of occupational trades.

For a few railroad industry leaders, benefits ranged from seats on interlocking boards of directors, to enormous equity holdings, to the kind of opulent lifestyles that gave substance to the title of the Gilded Age. From time to time, there might be efforts to rein in the railroads, but the railroad barons saw to it that new regulations were feeble, and laws were relatively toothless. Cheap labor was readily available, and railroads exploited that fact, eventually employing nearly 10 percent of the non-farm workforce in trades and occupations that often meant lifetime employment. One did not have to look very far to find someone connected to railroad activity.

Around the nation, established lines were extending spurs into new territory, small operations were being started up and promoters were advancing any number of ventures. For marginal railroad operators, the crash of 1893 a few years later drove many railroads toward acquisition-minded companies, if they survived at all. Established companies (Erie, Santa Fe, Union Pacific as notable examples) were also severely affected, prompting a wave of mergers and significant restructuring. It took another five years to reestablish a comfortable degree of stability.

In North Carolina, scores of railroad companies received permission to incorporate and receive their charters; only a fraction of them ever materialized. Far fewer of them managed to actually lay down tracks and become operational, however briefly.

This late-century wave of speculative ventures particularly affected secondary markets not well served by established railroads. Attention went to a town near the mouth of the Cape Fear River. Incorporated as Smithville, it was Brunswick County's largest town and county seat. Although it had only one thousand or so residents in the early 1880s, some thought it could be a major East Coast coal handling facility, perhaps recalling the concept from thirty years earlier. This enthusiasm prompted a renaming of the town to Southport in 1887 and thus led it to acquire a magnified perception of its importance, particularly as a coaling station.

Recent rechanneling of the Cape Fear River afforded deep-water capabilities for large ships drafting up to about twenty-five feet. If adequate coal handling facilities and a railhead could be established, the thinking went, the town would become a major stop on the Eastern Seaboard, and everyone there would share in an abundance of riches. In a steam-driven world, coal was king, and some dreamers saw Southport as a lucrative opportunity, fed by rail connections to inland coal fields.

At the time, most coal traveled to northern ports. However, for substantial coal deposits in lower Illinois and Indiana, Kentucky and Tennessee, the distance to port would be shorter with a southerly route to terminate somewhere along the mid-Atlantic coast. Shorter routes meant lower shipping costs to the producers, and a line that could capitalize on that would be able to draw a share of revenue away from northern railroads.

Western North Carolina also had vast hardwood forests being exploited by many logging operations and producers of cut lumber, shingles and siding, flooring and furniture, fuel and railroad ties (tens of millions needed annually). In addition, abundant mineral resources were being discovered, such as veins of abrasive corundum, feldspar for glass and ceramics, mica and many more. These also needed a path to market, and therein lay the rub.

The western region was served by only two railroads, both of which ran basically north and south to neighboring states. Products had to be moved, and existing carriers charged higher rates to move them for the relatively short distance out of North Carolina. To correct this inequality, or discrimination, western producers sought an east–west trunk route to the Atlantic for

> The issues of monopolistic practices and discriminatory rates (tariffs) are far too complex to be treated here. They were a constant source of complaints from producers and shippers. Suffice it to say that they were pervasive and persistent in national carriers, each of which devised its own schedule of rates, often supplemented by clandestine rebates and discounts. The situation began to brighten with passage of the Interstate Commerce Act of 1887 and the Sherman Antitrust Act of 1890, although that stimulated further creativity as railroads devised ways around the new regulations. In North Carolina, establishment of the North Carolina Railroad Commission provided a degree of rate control, although the table of rates quickly grew to a fearsome collection of highly detailed charges. Classes of products were constantly expanded, further subdivided among types of products within those classes, each with a specified rate according to measures of quantity, weight or volume.

southern coal fields, minerals and lumber from the region. Such a route would mean faster delivery to port, would alleviate the effects of monopolistic freight rate practices of established roads and would economically benefit a wide geographical belt across the southern part of North Carolina. (As vividly demonstrated west of the Mississippi River, it was seen that where the railroads ran, towns sprang up, commerce and agriculture flourished and significant economic benefits accrued to host states.)

Southport, as a "river" town and a "coastal" town, offered some intriguing possibilities as the terminus for a shorter route. After traversing the Appalachians (which affected all east–west railroads), a route to Southport came up as the most economical option to reach adequate harborage and to avoid entrenched existing carrier roads. In addition, transatlantic traffic, by shipping out at Southport, could avoid the treacherous waters off Cape Hatteras to the north. Of course, Southport had its own navigation peril to consider in the form of Frying Pan Shoals, extending several miles off the tip of Smith Island. The Cape Fear River kept a relatively stable channel between the shoals and the main shoreline, and deeper draft ships could safely navigate to Southport with the help of river pilots from the town. Nevertheless, those hazardous shallows claimed their share of shipwrecks along the Eastern Seaboard. As will be shown, plenty of exciting schemes were floated, with involvement of interests from as far away as Chicago, Philadelphia, Boston and New York.

Chapter 3

SURROUNDING RAIL DEVELOPMENTS

In the 1880s, the inspiration for Southport's excitement was found about twenty-five miles away, where railroads radiating out from Wilmington were actively engaged in their own corporate developments. The Wilmington & Weldon Railroad, begun in 1834, already controlled the Wilmington, Columbia & Augusta Railroad, the two of them providing northward and westward traffic from the Port City; think of them operating at the "nine o'clock" and "twelve o'clock" positions on a clock dial.

Growing alliances of the Wilmington & Weldon with railroads in Virginia, South Carolina, Georgia and Florida had already established an operating identity of an "Atlantic Coast Line" rail line. These alliances facilitated much faster north–south interstate transportation—certainly for freight (which paid the bills) but also for noteworthy passenger service. The participating railroads eventually would combine and formally establish the Atlantic Coast Line Railroad in 1900.

Likewise, the Carolina Central Railroad was aligning with other companies in much the same area, forming what would become Seaboard Air Line Railroad. From Wilmington, that company had run a straight-line tangent seventy-odd miles to Hamlet, occupying the "ten o'clock" position and effectively splitting the gap between the northward and westward Wilmington & Weldon and Wilmington, Columbia & Augusta routes. The Carolina Central also had an established presence in Wilmington and later (as Seaboard Air Line) would collaborate with the Atlantic Coast Line to finally bridge the branches of the Cape Fear River for a direct shot into the north end of the city.

> The rivalry between Seaboard Air Line and Atlantic Coast Line Railroads was an enduring thing, seeing as how they both provided mainline service in the region between the Piedmont and Atlantic coast. About seventy years later, they would merge, forming Seaboard Coast Line Railroad for several years. Seaboard's route to Hamlet is now owned by CSX Transportation, the ultimate successor of additional mergers and acquisitions. The other rail routes are long gone, leaving the CSX line as the sole track into Wilmington from inland areas.

Meanwhile, the Cape Fear & Yadkin Valley Railroad was operating its line toward Fayetteville and beyond, pretty much defining the "eleven o'clock" slot. It had some interest in extending its service to Southport, but that never seemed to progress beyond the correspondence stage. The company was continually beset with financial difficulties, and soon the portion to Fayetteville would be folded into the Atlantic Coast Line, while track beyond that was incorporated into Southern Railways. It was a gentlemen's agreement between chiefs of the two railroads, perhaps an example of now-forbidden market splitting.

Finally, there was the Wilmington, Onslow & East Carolina Railroad that operated from Wilmington in the "one o'clock" position toward Jacksonville, North Carolina, to the northeast. It, too, was soon driven to reorganize and become the Wilmington, New Bern & Norfolk Railroad. In a couple more years, it was drawn into the Atlantic Coast Line network to serve not only Jacksonville but also farther coastal communities like Havelock, Beaufort, Morehead City and up into Virginia.

Farther afield, J.P. Morgan was actively seeking to consolidate the Richmond & Danville, East Tennessee and Virginia & Georgia Railroads, among many others, into the Southern Railway system. Stretching along the Piedmont midlands, the system also provided trans-Appalachian routes, a factor that entered into many of the speculative schemes to connect inland areas to a terminus at Southport.

What was lacking was a line between Wilmington and Southport. That city, recently renamed from Smithville, had ambitions to become an important southern coastal port for commerce and leisure, perhaps to rival Wilmington, some twenty-five river miles upstream along the Cape Fear River. Such ambitions did not go unnoticed. Wilmington, already the terminus for several railroads, was determined not to be supplanted and actively developed its own competing prominence. In reaction to one of

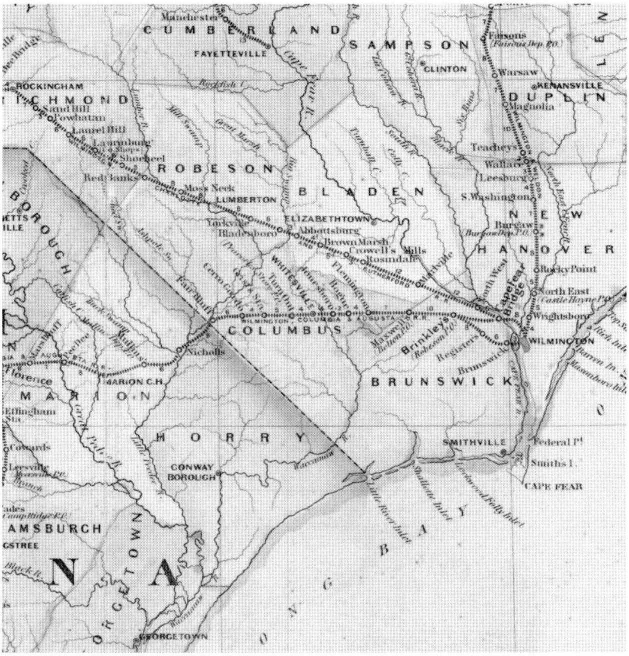

Through the 1870s, the railroads out of Wilmington were the Wilmington, Columbia & Augusta (west), Wilmington, Charlotte & Rutherford (northwest) and Wilmington & Weldon (north). By 1887, Smithville, at the mouth of the Cape Fear River, would change its name to Southport to show its ambition to become a major port on the Atlantic seaboard. *Asher & Adams, "North Carolina and South Carolina," detail, 1871. Courtesy of the State Archives of North Carolina.*

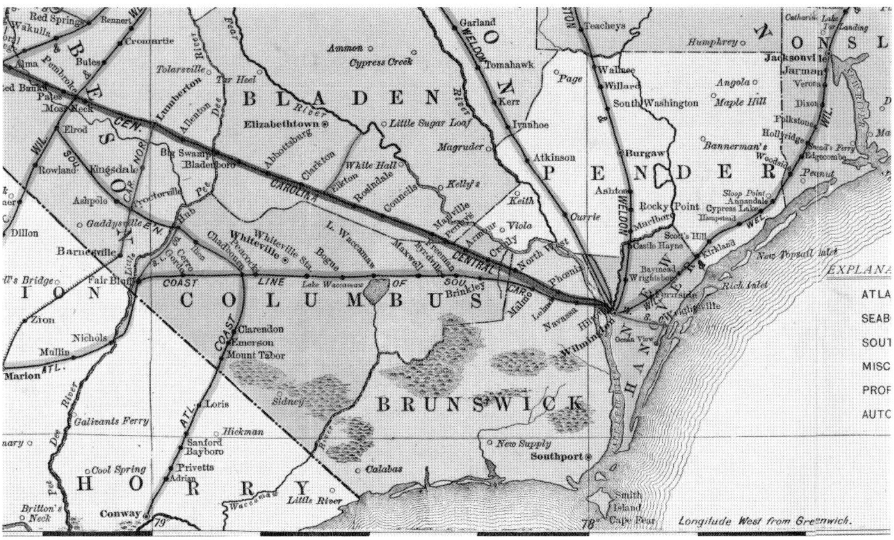

By 1900, five railroads radiated out from Wilmington in all directions except to the south, where there were exciting speculative ventures to develop Southport as a major coaling facility for transatlantic shipping. *Courtesy of the North Carolina Department of Natural and Cultural Resources. From Henry C. Brown, "Railroad Map of North Carolina," detail, North Carolina Corporation Commission/Rand McNally and Company, 1900.*

the earliest ventures, a rather peevish editorial in the *Wilmington Morning Star* of August 24, 1886, harrumphed:

> *We hear but little said of this contemplated road in Wilmington, but it looks to us that it would be very damaging to this town if it is built. If Wilmington sits still, holds its hands, and allows cities, towns, and villages not very remote to be put in communication by new routes of traffic with other sections, and does absolutely nothing to improve, increase or develop its own connections with the regions beyond, and it should find itself badly left, it will have itself to blame and not railroad companies.*

Much of what follows ultimately deals with connecting Southport and Wilmington, and some geographic context is likely needed. At the north end of the area of interest lay the city of Wilmington, situated on the Cape Fear River about thirty miles upstream from the open waters of the Atlantic Ocean. Although it enjoyed deep-water anchorage and was largely protected from Atlantic storms, it also was upstream from inconvenient shallows around the outflow of creeks along the river. About eleven miles to the southwest through forested and unpopulated land was Town Creek, nestled alongside the waterway by that name and on the colonial Wilmington-Georgetown Road. Between the two, additional settlements that would crop up were Woodruff, Leland, Lanvale, Easy Hill, El Paso and Bishop. Traveling another six miles south beyond Town Creek would take one through more forested and unpopulated land, with the settlements of Winnabow and (later) Bolivia. At this point, a bend to the southeast for fourteen miles would reach Smithville (Southport), with the eventual names of Loughlin, Goreville, Coolvale and Atwood in between. In terms of the clock dial analogy, the eventual route would strike out at "seven o'clock" from Wilmington and then bend to "five o'clock" at Bolivia.

Chapter 4

WHY SOUTHPORT?

At first glance, there would seem to be little to recommend Smithville (at the time) as a major port on the Atlantic coast. The village (laid out around a colonial-era fort) was platted for only one hundred or so lots and hemmed in by piney woods, coastal marsh and the Cape Fear River. It had been the county seat since 1808, assigned after the abandonment of Brunswick Town a few miles upriver.

During the Civil War, the town had been surrounded by impressive defenses, given its location at the entrance to the Cape Fear River with access to Wilmington and vital railheads in that city. Forts Caswell (just across the bay), Anderson (upriver on the site of the derelict Brunswick Town) and Fisher (the great coastal bulwark) were supplemented by an assortment of gun emplacements and batteries. For the most part, these were now all in ruins, if not totally disappeared. So Smithville reverted to a leisurely and quiet existence.

Smithville's 1880 population of about one thousand were largely occupied with river piloting, fishing and related goods and services. A few small merchants supplied provisions not available locally, and a smattering of boardinghouses accommodated seasonal workers and visitors. In the river, a quarantine station helped check the introduction of diseases arriving on ships or from infected seamen. The riverfront was very much a "working" stretch, with occasional piers, shoreline shanties, a sandy shallow beach to draw up boats or dry nets, pilots' structures and the like. What connection there was with the much larger city of Wilmington was by means of the river, since roads were so scarce and undependable throughout the mostly empty interior of the county.

The reputation of the fishing village was enduringly described as "quaint," with compliments about its friendly inhabitants and "salubrious breezes." Unpaved streets were perhaps "improved" with a crushed shell or clay/sand topcoat. Photographs from around the turn of the twentieth century suggest that parking wasn't much of a problem in downtown; vehicles were rare, and sometimes a horse and wagon would be left in the middle of the street while the owner conducted business. Drainage and curbs were absent, and sidewalks were apparently optional. Most streets were not only lined with trees, but the trees were actually in the streets, a situation that endures even today on many of the town's original secondary streets. At least until 1901, cows and other livestock roamed the town, foraging on whatever greenery they could find. Hardly the stuff of bold visions and speculation.

Most locals seemed to have felt just fine with the way things were in town. For outside interests, however, it was more the location than the character of Smithville that drew their attention as a potential shipping point for minerals and commodities from far inland. In their view, there were many positive attributes that had simply been overlooked (and undervalued) by the town's residents.

- Recently completed barriers across New Inlet and north of Smith's Island (Bald Head) confined the current of the Cape Fear River to scour out a reliable stretch of deep water along Southport's shore, enabling anchorage for larger seagoing vessels.

- Dredging where the Cape Fear River met the Atlantic Ocean provided a deeper channel across the bar and allowed larger ships of deeper draft to navigate safely into and out of the river.

- There was ample space along the riverfront to develop terminal and loading facilities.

- With facilities in Smithville, ships could avoid occasional river hazards when navigating up to and back from Wilmington, saving two days on their in-port stays.

- A railroad directly to Smithville would avoid entanglements with entrenched competition in Wilmington, which was already a terminus for five other railroads.

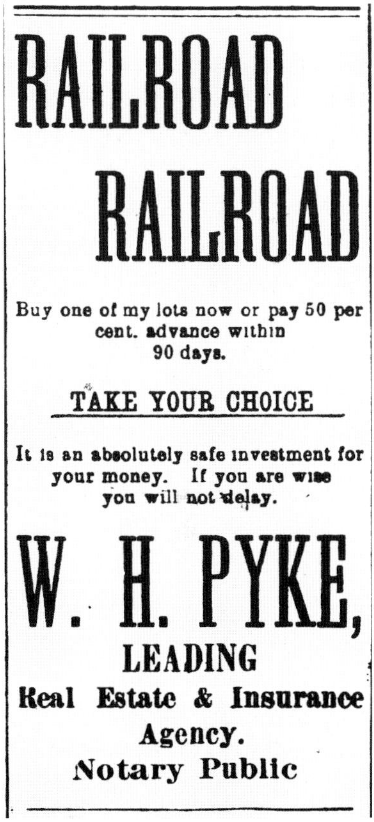

Left: An 1891 diagram of platted lots and parcels in Southport, showing the town's expansion (highlighted area) and doubling the amount of land available for development. *Courtesy of Southport Historical Society.*

Right: With the prospects of railroad prosperity, local realtors were quick to get properties to market. Southport Standard, *April 13, 1905.*

- For producers in western North Carolina and neighboring states, a route ending at Smithville meant faster shipping times to port. In addition, there was the potential for lucrative development along the route.

- Once through the Appalachians and Piedmont, rail construction was relatively inexpensive as the route traversed mostly flat land or gentle grades.

- Additional leisure and resort opportunities presented themselves with undeveloped Bald Head Island just a short boat trip away.

Once the spotlight was turned on, Smithville became much livelier. Additional blocks for development were platted out, doubling its size. Riverfront parcels suddenly became more valuable. City aldermen and county commissioners were diving into the realms of franchise grants and bond issues. The practice of speculative real estate became much more active, along with the importance of clarifying who owned what. The city's population grew in anticipation of the benefits of commerce, whether commercial and mercantile or for the leisure trade.

The excitement was infectious. By 1887, the town had changed its name to Southport, reflecting its ambitions. Two or three speculative railroad ventures were already percolating. Far-away interests in Chicago, Boston, Philadelphia and Baltimore were actively weighing the prospects of a new major port between Norfolk, Virginia, and Charleston, South Carolina. Surveyors and railroad company representatives were eagerly promoting their views in towns and counties along their projected routes.

And the fun was just beginning.

Chapter 5

PERSISTENCE OF VISION

Around the mouth of the Cape Fear River, there was plenty of enthusiasm about railroad development. Speculators laid out any number of ideas whereby rails could be laid to a terminal at the ocean, and Smithville emerged as the closest possibility. For North Carolina, this also meant a new source of revenue from an additional railroad and port fees. As noted, Smithville caught the railroad fever and changed its name to Southport amid much excitement. A typical chest-thumping editorial in the *Southport Leader* (November 12, 1891) colorfully proclaimed the benefits of railroad development:

> *Brunswick County has had for over thirty years a hard struggle in the race of life, laboring under the disadvantage and inconvenience of being shut off from the rest of the world for the want of cheap transportation and communication….*
>
> *The hour of Brunswick's deliverance has come, Southport will be the great seaport of the South which nature always intended it should be, so rally around the banner of progress, connect Southport with Chicago, and Brunswick will yet be the richest County in the state.*

Many of these visions saw Southport as a major coaling stop for shipping on the Eastern Seaboard—provided, of course, that some way could be found to get coal to Southport in the first place. The major obstacle was the geographic challenge of the Appalachians. A number of short lines were already operating there; perhaps they could be pieced together for a more continuous route. Quite a number of ventures were being promoted late in the nineteenth century, ranging from poor to awful. Thanks to telegraphic wire services, newspapers throughout the state and beyond dutifully reported on their appearance and progress (or lack thereof). Nearly all of them remained ephemeral and never gained much traction. The names of these ventures reflected where their aspirations lay.

- South Atlantic & Ohio: Only a blip, but first out of the gate in 1881, this venture sought to connect a mining company in Wise County, Virginia, with Smithville (Southport). It could run its trains for part of the distance on the tracks of existing railroads, threading their way through the Appalachians and Piedmont. It was estimated that only 120 miles of inexpensive new road, mostly through coastal flats and lowlands, would have to be built out of the 400-mile distance.

- South Atlantic & Northwestern: Proposed in 1886 while the city was still Smithville (but not for long), the idea was to lay a road to Bristol, a bifurcated junction town straddling the Tennessee and Virginia state lines, some four hundred miles distant. A subsequent modification would link to Tennessee railroads all the way to Memphis in what may have been an attempt to connect with the Mississippi River and its great traffic in commodities. (Such a scheme would also allow steamboats to avoid the many shifting and time-consuming twists and turns and sandbars of the lower Mississippi.) A railroad with a relatively straight shot to the Atlantic coast could get commodity shipments there much faster. By loading on the East Coast instead of the Gulf Coast, vessels could also avoid the route around the Florida peninsula. Commodity traders from the Chicago Board of Trade were apparently backing the venture, seeing it as a way to reduce the domineering influence of the New York Central and Pennsylvania Railroads to Northeast ports or to avoid the extra time shipping out of New Orleans and into the Gulf of Mexico. As an added bonus when trains were making vacation travel more accessible, the undeveloped seashore in North Carolina offered untapped leisure potential beyond the movement of freight. (They apparently took a page from Henry Flagler's playbook, where he had his railroad built to develop the beaches of Florida as vacation hotspots. Resort and tourist travel were becoming popular, and the beaches of North Carolina were ripe targets for development. Southport, along with nearby Smith's Island (or Bald Head Island, as it is now known), provided outstanding commercial and leisure possibilities.) Much excitement attended the proposal in the Carolina counties through which the line would run, and the rationale continued to permeate successive ventures. Brunswick County voters were enormously excited by the prospects, and they enthusiastically approved $100,000 in bonds to support it. However, the venture had considerably more difficulty in obtaining enough subscriptions among the other North Carolina counties along the route, and it quickly went through a major reorganization. A revival was attempted in 1887, but the company did not begin work by 1890. Despite some willingness by the county commissioners to make allowances for the company, the bond subscription eventually was revoked. The effort lingered on a couple of years more as some properties were optioned or bought near the Cape Fear River. A subsidiary, the Southport Construction Company, was formed by some of the railroad principals to handle construction, but that effort did not get very far either. That company was succeeded for the same project by the Cape Fear Harbor & Coal Company, just in time for the great 1893 financial panic to deal a final blow to the enterprise. Another actor, the Cape Fear Coaling & Contracting Company, undertook to build docks, wharves, buildings and handling facilities at the river, but that, too, succumbed to larger economic forces.

William Weeks, a major Southport property holder, got involved in 1892 with the Southport Construction Company, the outfit that was formed to build the South Atlantic & Northwestern. Apparently, he was such an ardent believer in railroads that he took his mules and dragpan and regularly graded some surveyed roadway on his own and for no pay. Precisely where he did this is uncertain, but piney woods closely abutted the edge of built-up Southport, and perhaps he worked along its margins. In addition to real estate, he maintained his interests in various successive railroad ventures until his death in 1910.

- The Northern & Southern North Carolina Railroad Company: This company was one of twenty-seven railroads incorporated in the state in 1887; it was the earliest to describe a fallback proposal for a limited road just from Smithville to already-established railroad connections at Wilmington (expansion presumably would come later). The company rented the Pavilion in Smithville for railroad offices and planned to build wharves near the Hotel Brunswick, and it requested that the name of the town be Southport, which was accomplished in March.

- Wilmington & Southport (Southern?): This apparently never got beyond the chartering stage in 1891, although it was allowed to sell stock. It continued with the modest and perhaps more realistic goal of simply running from Southport to Wilmington, which became an abiding feature of subsequent proposals. Some confusion remains about the name of the company—Southern or Southport. In any event, the venture led nowhere, and its charter was eventually sold to Brunswick, Southern & Western (below).

- Cape Fear & Cincinnati: Simultaneously with the previous venture (and overlapping the difficult final years of the South Atlantic & Northwestern), this new company ambitiously envisioned a line from Southport to Wilmington and also from Southport westward to Florence, South Carolina, and then north to Salisbury, North Carolina. Further developments had the line branch off between Conway and Camden, South Carolina, where it would diverge in directions toward Georgetown and Charleston and westward toward Chester, South Carolina, and Shelby, North Carolina, thence to Knoxville or Chattanooga, Tennessee. In 1890, as reported by the *Wilmington Morning Star*, this venture went so far as to form the Massachusetts Construction Company to build the line, where some riverfront facilities were already owned. Baltimore and Boston interests were now behind the venture, but this also failed because Brunswick County was still considering its $100,000 approved bonds for the failing South Atlantic & Northwestern, which was continuing to play for time during its troubles. The effort also stimulated the formation of factions in town, complicating its efforts to successfully establish a position. The company had better success drumming up interest in South

With multiple railroads working at the same time to secure franchises and development rights, it was inevitable that local factions would develop to support one or another of them. Margaret Coit Curtis, who was married to Dr. Walter Curtis (attending physician at the quarantine station), kept a diary from 1886 to 1896. Besides regular entries lamenting the lack of progress on getting a railroad (they had purchased a hotel in anticipation of passenger traffic), she provided insights about a few of the local railroad activists and how they were maneuvering to gain advantage in the ventures.

Carolina (where the concept was a novel idea) but could not effectively withstand a series of procedural problems and delays in North Carolina. This seems to have been a recurring situation in the early ventures. With all the tub-thumping enthusiasm by outsiders for establishing Southport as the terminus for far-inland shipments, intervening counties saw few enrichments for their own interests.

• As reported in the *Wilmington Messenger*, a railroad survey team was rumored to be working its way up the west bank of the Cape Fear River in November 1891. The party was supposedly backed by the Baltimore & Ohio Railroad, although it is unknown whether it was on behalf of any of the existing players in the area. This may have been related to the putative effort to attract the B&O as a player in the development efforts.

• Brunswick Western & Southern: Incorporated in 1891, this company purchased the charter of the Wilmington & Southport (or Southern?) to connect Southport to Wilmington. In a common practice among railroad companies, this was to be built in 1892 by its subsidiary Cape Fear Harbor & Coal Company, a survivor of the fiasco with the South Atlantic & Northwestern. At the north end, the line would be built out from either Seaboard Air Line or Atlantic Coast Line tracks at Meares Bluff (now Navassa) to Southport and from there bend west into South Carolina and up to Knoxville, Tennessee. Besides coal, potential revenue sources included commodities shipments from Chicago markets, where the distance to an ocean port was calculated to be about 160 miles shorter to Southport than shipping to northern ports. Some local enthusiasm resurfaced when this venture was promoted, but local backers quickly sold to Chicago interests. A $100,000 stock-for-bonds swap was proposed for Brunswick County but failed, as did a company promise to hire Southport labor if Southport by itself backed $25,000 in bonds. Voters were likely becoming leery about all the speculation. The nascent company did purchase some 215 acres of land with river frontage in Southport, probably the holdings of the earlier Cape Fear & Cincinnati. The company ordered up eighty thousand crossties and started construction at the northern end of the line, using its subsidiary (now the Southport Construction Company) to execute the work. The bank panic of 1893 pretty well crushed progress on this endeavor, too.

- Southport & Western: In 1895, this fleeting company tried to obtain $59,000 in bond support from Brunswick County townships instead of the county itself. Ultimately, it was unable to get a proper start on construction, and the company disappeared.

- Carolina, Tennessee & Ohio: Now Philadelphia interests got involved with the effort. They got this company chartered in 1895, and it began a brief but eventful existence. It purchased all the effects of the defunct Brunswick Western & Southern, including the large tract for access to 2,800 feet of riverfront at the southern terminus of a proposed line between Southport and Wilmington. Coal was expected to be shipped from the Cunnock fields in Pennsylvania and Pocahontas fields in West Virginia, and there were further

The failings of the South Atlantic & Northwestern led some Southport residents to pool their properties in a speculative bid to sell to another railroad, and they contacted the Baltimore & Ohio, whose agent came to Southport to begin the process. When he left town to get commitments from the B&O, however, parties from the South Atlantic & Northwestern quietly bought up options on several of those properties and a riverfront parcel, intending to convey them to their quickly formed Southport Construction Company. Upon his return, the B&O's agent realized that his pooling arrangement had been undercut, and a few contentious meetings led to a complete collapse of these ventures.

expectations for commodity shipments like corn, wheat and cotton. At the north end, the route was being built out at Meares Bluff (Navassa) by the Union Construction Company, using about a mile and a half right-of-way of a long-gone railroad (Wilmington & Manchester) and clearing by the Brunswick Western & Southern a couple of years earlier. Work was proceeding southward toward Town Creek with grading and trestle building and a workforce of about two hundred men. In July, colorful descriptions in the *Wilmington Messenger* depicted scenes of great activity and plans to lay track at the rate of a mile a day. About eight miles of roadbed and some bridges were completed, and the principals were ready to "go shopping" for crossties and rails. However, a few months later, the bank and money crises of 1896 led to the company being placed in receivership. Its assets (franchise, roadbed, right-of-way, culverts, bridges and the like) were sold in 1897 for a mere $10,000 to the next contender.

The Wilmington Messenger (January 1892) reported that the Brunswick Western & Southern put a down payment on Bald Head Island, which was sold to the railroad company for $25,000. Promoters had ideas for a grand resort hotel with many amenities and the island itself becoming a "paradise" for visitors. The company also floated the idea of renaming the island for George Pullman, president of the Pullman Palace Car Company. Pullman already owned Castle Rest, a small personal island in the St. Lawrence River. Perhaps the promoters of the South Atlantic & Northwestern thought he could be persuaded to invest in their venture if he could also acquire a branded resort island. In any event, the proposal went nowhere; the Pullman company had other issues brewing that would come to a head the following year.

• Southport Terminal Railroad: Two or three parties from the Carolina, Tennessee & Ohio formed this company, with an investor base of about two dozen individuals. In its brief life, it intended to construct, maintain and operate a railroad between Southport and Wilmington. It was able to secure some rights-of-way in Town Creek Township along surveyed lines from previous companies. Logging operations already existed in the area, and it is likely there were tramways that could be adapted to railroad use.

- Cape Fear Terminal Railroad: In 1899, local interests briefly took up where the Carolina, Tennessee & Ohio left off. Apparently backed by Seaboard Air Line, its intentions were to build from Southport to Wilmington and also toward Seaboard's trunk line in Bladen County.

- Southport, Wilmington & Western: A little later, a group of about two dozen Philadelphia investors spearheaded the formation of this company in 1899, which may have been a buyout of the Cape Fear Terminal interests. Projections echoed the earlier bright prospects for Southport, in this case as the end of a connected chain of eight to twelve railroads stretching inland to Kentucky. In September, the *Raleigh Farmer & Mechanic* continued to bang the drum for a major trunk line, editorializing, "Southport, as is well known, has one of the very best deep water harbors on the South Atlantic coast. To suppose that it will be made merely the terminus of a local short road hauling from Wilmington to Southport is to sadly overlook the possibilities of the situation." Additional surveying was done, and the Southport Board of Aldermen granted right-of-way development between Moore Street and the Cape Fear River for future terminal facilities, mostly on the parcels that had already been earmarked for development. In 1901, the company's charter was repealed since it failed to start construction as promised.

- A letter to the editor of the *Southport Standard* (March 22, 1900) outlined the concept of a Tennessee Eastern & Western railroad to be built by interests from Ohio. The extraordinary proposal saw the route from Southport to Knoxville, Tennessee, as the easternmost link in a railroad that stretched to Omaha, Nebraska.

> *ANOTHER RAILROAD ~~ Col. Boone Writes of His Plans for a Line to Southport ~~ Zanesville. O. March 19, 1900 ~~* [To] *Mr. E.B. Stevens, Southport, N.C. ~~ Sir: I have the pleasure of stating that I am laying my plans to build a railroad from the coal fields west of Knoxville to Southport, N.C. and at the same time to make it a link in a chain of railroads from Omaha, Neb. to Southport, N.C. via Knoxville, Tenn., line to cross the Mississippi River at Louisiana, Mo. and the Ohio River at Owensboro,*

Ky. A line of railroad from Knoxville, Tenn. to Southport, N.C., about 495 miles in length, will also act as the seaboard outlet for the Tennessee Eastern and Western when built.... I project the line to pass through South Carolina via Marion, Florence, Camden, Winnsboro and Greenville. The line could be taken through South Carolina via Bennettville, Chesterfield, Lancaster, Chester, and Spartanburg. Which route will furnish the most local traffic as well as through traffic to Southport? Railroad building is a business, and not a sentimental affair, but for all that, a railroad which has the friendship of the people through whose lands it runs, will, everything else being equal, have a material advantage over a corporation which has the enmity of the people.—Albert F. Boone

- Southport, Wilmington & Durham: Incorporated in 1901, this was the latest in what was becoming a lengthy list of aspirants. The company negotiated with local interests to take over the now-defunct Southport, Wilmington & Western (itself the successor of three previous efforts), including thirty-eight acres of riverfront property on which to build terminal facilities. It was intended to connect with the Norfolk & Western trunk through Durham and thence to coal fields in Virginia and West Virginia. The *Wilmington Messenger* reported that, to keep its charter alive, it actually began construction work—four days before the deadline expired in 1903. By 1905, it was summoned to court for fraud and to name a receiver for its assets, which were sold for only $10,000 to satisfy claims.

- Just a blip in the record, 1899 saw the incorporation of the Southport & Western Railroad. It is unknown if this was an attempt to resurrect the earlier road of the same name (1895) or was an independent launch of a new company.

- The first few years of the twentieth century got very confused as many companies were chartered that saw Southport as a valuable terminal town. (Perhaps this was fueled by a healthy dose of turn-of-the-century optimism as the calendar turned over to the 1900s.) In North Carolina between 1899 and 1905, at least eighty railroads were chartered, the previous Southport & Western Railroad among them. In a bewildering list of easily confused names, these years saw the Southport & Western Railway;

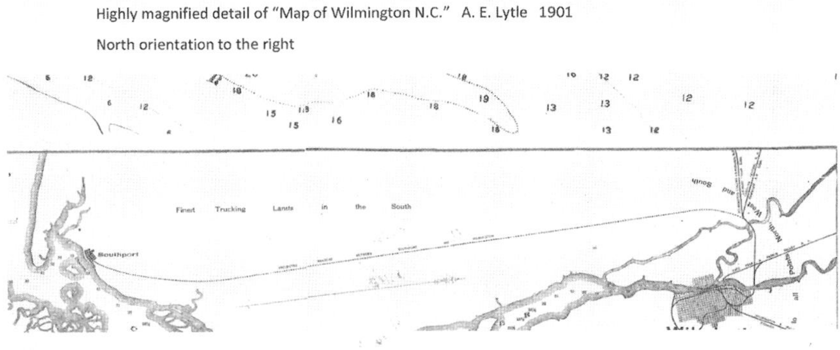

By 1900, there were enough previous attempts and interest in a Southport-to-Wilmington railroad to develop a speculative map. Here in its earliest form, the route is simply laid out as a straight line from Navassa to Southport. This was for purposes of illustration, rather than being grounded in actual conditions. Note that north is to the right. *A.E. Lytle, "Map of Wilmington N.C.," detail, Union Map and Atlas Co., 1901. Courtesy of the North Carolina Department of Natural and Cultural Resources.*

Southport & Northwestern; Raleigh & Southport; Southport Northern & Western; Southport Atlantic & Northwestern; Southport, Wilmington & Durham; Southport Atlantic & Western; and Southport & Atlantic Terminal. Just to keep things interesting, rumors were floating about bigger railroads backing some of these efforts, such as the Baltimore & Ohio, Chesapeake & Ohio, Seaboard Air Line, Pennsylvania, Southern, Cape Fear & Yadkin Valley and the Atlantic Coast Line.

- Southport, Atlantic & Northern: In 1905, this company acquired nearly eight hundred acres of riverfront land, including the thirty-eight acres from the now-defunct Southport, Wilmington & Durham. The *Wilmington Morning Star* noted the existence of several railroad companies with various privileges into Southport, along with four new companies chartered by the North Carolina General Assembly.

- South Atlantic Terminal Company: In 1905, this company also aimed to build a railway to Wilmington. Given that some surveying, grading and trestle building had been done almost ten years earlier, this would likely have been an effort to connect fragments of the earlier Southport, Wilmington & Western, whose charter had been repealed. The company went so far as to acquire right-of-way permissions from many local landowners. As reported by the *Polk County News*, the $150,000 in stock was nearly all held by H.H. Dougherty of New York, who by that time had been active in the area for more than ten years in several earlier railroad ventures.

- Raleigh & Southport (or Raleigh & Cape Fear): This was pretty much an outsider company, only running from Raleigh to Lillington, North Carolina, at the time. The company issued additional stock and aspired to extend the line to Southport but only got as far as Fayetteville. A struggle arose among railroad companies over the route between Fayetteville and Wilmington (the defunct Cape Fear & Yadkin Valley Railroad), but the Raleigh & Southport was not the winner. In 1911, it was purchased by the Norfolk Southern Railroad of that time, with the contested route being acquired by the Atlantic Coast Line.

- South Atlantic & Transcontinental: In 1906, this was the last "grand scheme" to establish Southport as a terminus for the coal fields of eastern Tennessee and points much farther away. Promotion was by a Colonel S.A. Jones of Waynesville, North Carolina, who had moved to the state in 1894 from Tampa, Florida. For the next several years, Jones lined up testimonials and resolutions of support from state houses, chambers of commerce, business associations and counties for a line from Knoxville, Tennessee, to Southport. Counties in western North Carolina were particularly keen on the project, seeing relief from discriminatory freight rates imposed by the few railroads serving the area. Time and distance advantages could also be extended to producers in eastern Tennessee and Kentucky. A map purported to show how the proposed line would cut across north–south trunk lines to establish a more direct (and shorter) route to the ocean. It was hoped that the project would alleviate the sore point of freight rates imposed by railroads that already had a lock on coal hauling. The company was taken over by others and renamed in 1912. Due to legal problems and deaths of principals, the project faltered in 1913, although Jones was pushing the concept as late as 1920.

Left: The distinguished "Colonel" S.A. Jones (1852–1933) of Waynesville, North Carolina, who advocated an east–west trunk line through North Carolina with a terminus at Southport. He vigorously lobbied in several states to support and endorse the line. Although he was ultimately unsuccessful, it took him over ten years to drop the proposal. North Carolinian, *August 24, 1899.*

Below: Map of the proposed route of the South Atlantic and Transcontinental, as proposed by Colonel S.A. Jones. The road would cut across existing north–south railroads to end at Southport as a new competitive seaport. Never one to think small, Jones charted out a theoretical reach as far as Winnipeg, Canada, some 1,700 miles away! Asheville Gazette-News, *January 19, 1911.*

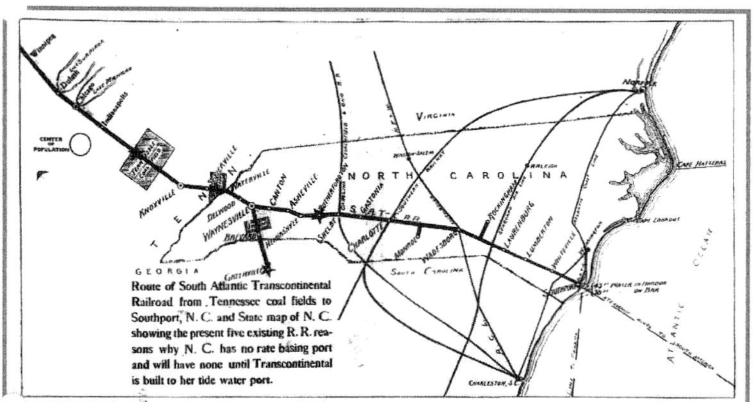

- Cape Fear, Southport & Atlantic Railroad: In 1907, this company made only a brief appearance, with intentions of running a track from Southport to Wilmington. Although it obtained some right-of-way permissions, it never proceeded beyond that stage.

During this period, Southport transitioned from a small village to a larger village. New blocks had been platted, and the town doubled the number of residences standing—to 260 from about 125. From 1890 to 1910, about 300 more people were added to the population, bringing the total to 1,484 at the 1910 census. As detailed by Landmark Preservation

Associates in *Comprehensive Historical/Architectural Site Survey of Brunswick County, North Carolina* (2010), a developing commercial district saw a new lumber company for structural and finish materials, and a brick and tile company furnished products to construct more permanent buildings downtown. However, the town still had trees growing in its streets, it was still hemmed in by its historical geographic features and it was nowhere near the dream of prominence declared by railroad speculators.

Construction of the Panama Canal (1904–14) provided fresh impetus to ideas of port development. If Southport was a desirable terminus, Panama was due south and offered the shortest route to the Pacific Ocean (including the detour around Cuba, which affected all shipping). By this time, however, attention was more centered on a modest rail link from Southport to Wilmington, where existing rail facilities made for a more realistic connection than a new trunk line toward the Appalachians. A coal dock had been built in Southport, although it seems to have been an unlovely affair, supported by a forest of timber piles braced against the river current and tides. In later years, a grainy and poorly inked newspaper photo shows a few cars on the pier, which appears to be connected to a one-ship wharf. Its use would be almost entirely connected with occasional "topping off" of coal for steamships, rather than as a large loading platform for major outbound shipments. The allure of a prominent coaling station seems to have cooled off. Instead, local industry pivoted toward maritime trades, fishing and fish processing as several operations were established in the area.

For most of the attempted railroad ventures so far, there seemingly was relatively little attention paid to business that could be generated locally; instead, the focus was on end-point facilities for outgoing bulk interstate shipments. The sparseness of Brunswick County's population did little to inspire great promises of home-grown commerce. In 1900, the county's population was 12,567, which, when apportioned among the county's 850 square miles deemed as "land" (and that mostly forested), averaged only 15 people per square mile.

Two decades of financial crises had already driven waves of mergers and acquisitions among railroads, where those in shaky circumstances were forced out of business or, if blessed with strength in their service areas, were absorbed into larger companies. Launching a major railroad start-up, such as that once envisioned for Southport in more robust times, was increasingly untenable. Despite larger aspirations, the concept had to be scaled back to become a small-scale operator in the larger industry.

S.A. Jones (1853–1933) seems to have led an interesting life, according to news reports of his exploits. He settled in burgeoning Tampa from Kentucky (with a short stint in Oklahoma) in the 1880s. Although he was a lawyer, he began as a carpenter and soon established a busy building supply business and became a real estate power. Together with a partner, he crafted deals for subdivisions and rapid expansion of that city with its exploitation of major phosphate deposits nearby. Some of the other causes he espoused were the building of decent surface roads, promoting a Nicaraguan canal instead of the Panamanian one and monetary reform in the manner of William Jennings Bryan. As his influence grew, he added the honorific "Colonel," and his paths crossed with Henry Flagler and Henry Plant, regional railroad magnates who were exploiting commercial and leisure opportunities in Florida. After contracting malaria while surveying in the Everglades, he moved to Waynesville, North Carolina, for his health in the 1890s. There he became very busy in mining and minerals, which he managed until his death in 1933 at the age of eighty-one. He was an intensely persuasive lobbyist, getting endorsements for his railroad venture from many state assemblies, governors, county boards, communities and chambers of commerce. A former newspaper editor, he was a prodigious writer to local newspapers, publishing exhaustively detailed letters running to thousands of words and filling many columns. In later years, he was again active around Tampa, advocating for industrial development and a trans-Florida canal. (There may be material for an interesting biographical study, if anyone chooses to do so.)

These successive efforts fitfully approached what would be the final form of a rail route between Southport and Wilmington. Earliest was the choice of Southport as a terminus, with (ultimately unworkable) trunk-line routes that would extend as far inland as Tennessee (or farther). Then, instead of laying a new road over hundreds of miles, the practicality of joining up with existing routes near Wilmington became evident. To lock in the Southport terminus, the Brunswick Western & Southern acquired riverfront parcels (and other companies in succession). Surveying and some preliminary work started on the route, although that moved forward in irregular stages. Along the way, there were the transient and ephemeral

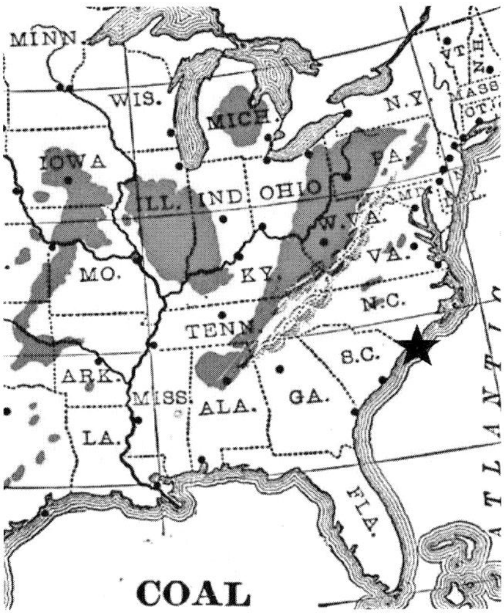

Detail from a map of United States coal fields. Production from the southern fields (Kentucky and Tennessee) would have a shorter trip to Southport (*star*) than taking more northerly routes across Ohio and Pennsylvania. A relatively low gap in the Appalachians (roughly where U.S. Highway 19E runs today) points directly to Southport. *"Coal,"* Frye's First Steps in Geography *(Boston: Ginn & Co., 1906).*

proposals, complete with reorganizations and buyouts, all afflicted by periodic upheavals in capital markets.

During this period and into the 1910s, the rather grand "mission" of a railroad, i.e., to establish Southport as a major coaling station on the Eastern Seaboard, was repeatedly floated. However, it was also successively deferred until the contemplated railroad itself became more of a feeder spur for established trunk lines out of Wilmington. In essence, the times had moved beyond the capability of interests to fulfill the vision, and the railroad idea, now more than twenty years in forming, had been reduced to increasingly modest proportions. This was a first element in limiting the outlook for a new railroad company: it simply could not find an effective place among entrenched and consolidating competitors, and what local traffic there was would never sustain an independent operation.

But the show had to go on.

Chapter 6

GREAT EXPECTATIONS

As we have seen, successive efforts fitfully approached the form of a rail route between Southport and Wilmington. Repeated promises of much larger projects rang hollow, and financial crises eroded the confidence and risk tolerance of sources of capital. Nearby railroads (notably the Atlantic Coast Line and Seaboard Air Line) were able to weather the financial storms somewhat better, and they continued to strengthen their presence. For more than twenty years, some two dozen ideas and proposals had at least intended to secure Southport's place among the several significant ports up and down the Eastern Seaboard. In a bewildering stew of similar-sounding names, they included the following.

- Companies that were able to execute original construction of some significance, whether at the north end or the south end or in the middle around Town Creek: South Atlantic & Northwestern (1886), Cape Fear & Cincinnati (1890), Brunswick Western & Southern (1891), Carolina, Tennessee & Ohio (1896), Southport Terminal Railroad (1896).

- Companies that more or less held on to progress to date, perhaps with some small additional improvements: Wilmington & Southport (1891), Cape Fear Terminal Railroad (1899), Southport, Wilmington & Western (1899), South Atlantic Terminal Co. (1905).

- Companies that got charters or sprouted up but went nowhere: South Atlantic & Ohio (1881); Northern & Southern North Carolina (1887); Southport & Western Railroad (1896); Southport & Western Railway; Southport & Northwestern; Southport Northern & Western; Southport Atlantic & Northwestern; Southport, Wilmington & Durham; Southport Atlantic & Western; Southport & Atlantic Terminal; Cape Fear, Southport & Atlantic; Southport & Western; Southport Atlantic & Northern; Raleigh & Southport (1905); South Atlantic & Transcontinental (1906); Southport Southern & Western (1907).

By now, the times had moved beyond the grand vision of new interstate trunk lines linking areas of production with a new international port. The railroad idea had been scaled back more than 90 percent to much more modest goals, and it could be safely presumed that the appetite for public underwriting of all these ventures had evaporated. If a line was to be built, it likely would be a railroad by the local business community for the benefit of local trade, rather than another major line out of southeastern North Carolina.

Instead of being a terminus for seabound coal and commodities, Southport's fortunes were increasingly defined by local fish processing. Several factories had been established, with at least a couple of them floating, to produce tons and tons of fish byproducts to supplement the harvests of shrimp, oysters and desirable fish. This also required facilities to make ice, used for fresh products for long trips in railcars. Presumably, the processors were counting on the eventual arrival of a railroad to quickly and efficiently carry their products to inland markets. Until that time, they had to temporarily rely on river transport to Wilmington railheads or conventional seagoing transportation.

With times ripe for consolidating progress, private interests closer to home, instead of faraway speculators, seemed ready to take it on. In 1905, three businessmen with deep interests in timber and lumber south of Fayetteville met to plan a strategy to tap into the enormous forest potential in Brunswick County. Two of them also had experience with short-line railroads operating around Fayetteville. Later that year, these entrepreneurs purchased and improved an existing sawmill operation at Town Creek, about twelve miles outside Wilmington toward Southport. The Brunswick County Register of Deeds noted that purchase price was $50,000 for all acreage, mill and assorted buildings, equipment and tools, livestock, locomotive, tracks and ancillary appurtenances.

To the last group might be added the Norfolk, Wilmington & Charleston Railroad of 1891. When it showed up, it caused a good deal of confusion; after all, there were already three other railroad companies vying for support at the time. A flurry of news dispatches quickly made the rounds, describing an improbable network joining Norfolk, Virginia, with Charleston, South Carolina, via Wilmington, Southport and Conway, South Carolina. Claims were made about purchasing railroad lines that didn't exist or lines that hadn't yet been built. Curiously, Wilmington and Southport were completely bypassed on the mapped route. The extraordinary description went on to depict trunk lines to the west connecting to interior states—all to be accomplished in about three years. The story was soon debunked, and the company disappeared.

The owner of the mill, one R.W. Gibson, had built it in 1903 to produce cut lumber and shingles, drawing from about three thousand forested acres he owned in the area. Gibson also built a tram rail line to penetrate his acreage for logging. Any of this infrastructure would have been cheaply built and not meant to endure—native logs might be used as crossties and laid directly on a graded path. The Town Creek operation likely would have used mules to pull logs from where they were felled; a serviceable locomotive hauled loaded cars on primitive tram tracks to the sawmill. Here, the finished product would be floated down Town Creek to the Cape Fear River or perhaps loaded onto wagons for a laborious trek to the north or south. Gibson likely would have used rights-of-way in Town Creek township awarded to the Southport Terminal Railroad in 1898.

With the purchase, the new owners formed the Town Creek Railroad & Lumber Company. They purchased the entire Gibson mill and its holdings: owned acreage, machinery, buildings, livestock, equipment, tramways, tools, steam barge and a wood-burning locomotive of unknown provenance. As recorded by the Brunswick County Register of Deeds, they quickly (and quietly) set about gaining access to marketable timber on at least forty-four more parcels of land. In total, they spent or obligated more than $100,000 for harvesting rights on about twenty-five thousand acres. (For comparison, the city of Southport at the time probably held fewer than five hundred acres of land within its boundaries.) Besides acquiring these "timber deeds," as they were called, they also got permission for one-hundred-foot right-of-way strips from over sixty landowners along an expected route. The typical arrangement awarded landowners undescribed benefits by virtue of having the railroad run through their property, plus cash consideration of one dollar. This included the northern several miles of old roadbed of the defunct Carolina, Tennessee & Ohio from ten years earlier.

Their plan called for extracting and processing logs from a swath of parcels about seventeen miles long and two to three miles wide straddling a rough line from Town Creek to beyond Supply. These holdings contained an estimated hundred million board feet of pine and cypress, along with twenty-five to thirty million board feet of hardwoods, all virgin timber, according to the *Wilmington Messenger* of January 1, 1907. Revenues from these operations would presumably subsidize the expense of constructing a railroad line, and the sooner, the better—at least $100,000 had already been paid or obligated for timber rights. The company also owned several thousand cleared acres for truck produce.

They formally incorporated the operation in 1907, drawing in additional investors with a stock capitalization of $250,000. They also formed and incorporated a subsidiary, the Wilmington, Brunswick & Southern Railroad (WB&S), authorized for $200,000 in stock. This company would set out to achieve the ultimate goal of improving and connecting previous fragments from Navassa southward to at least the recently established town of Bolivia (roughly the route of U.S. Highway 17 today). With some of the preliminary work accomplished and paid for by earlier failed attempts, putting it all together would be fairly inexpensive.

Tactically, the Town Creek company, with tens of thousands of forest and agriculture acres under its control, would then have both a northern outlet near Wilmington and southern terminus at Southport for logging and sawmill operations along the line. Fortunately, earlier ventures had surveyed much of the inland route, albeit in piecemeal fashion. Trying to strike a straight line (and the shortest distance) to Southport from Navassa along the river was impractical. That would have involved many estuarine creeks and marshes, privately held shoreline plantations and expensive miles-long plunges through virgin territory. Instead, a route was plotted more or less following the old colonial Wilmington-Georgetown Road, which at least had the advantage of having been reliably established for over one hundred years. From various points along the road, survey teams could pack in a short distance to stake out a rough route, and fine-tuning could wait until the various segments approached one another during the process of clearing and grading. They were able to conveniently stitch together the "easy parts," at least as far as Bolivia.

> Although it had some promising prospects, the Town Creek operation had its own troubles over the years. It never paid dividends on its stock; indeed, director Z.W. Whitehead brought suit in 1914 against the company for this and other actions bordering on malfeasance. At issue were the actions of two of Town Creek's officers, who partnered to form a separate shingle company and then surreptitiously deeded several thousand acres of the lumber company's land to it. The shingle company then sold its product back to Town Creek, which had to borrow to make the purchases. The officers essentially paid themselves from Town Creek borrowings, as filtered through their shingle company. The Town Creek operation made no money, was $114,000 in debt and had deteriorating facilities. With new owners, the company was placed in receivership in 1917, and it sold thousands of acres of land or timber rights to stay afloat. In 1919, its plant burned down, but the company was resurrected in 1920 with a new mill under another new ownership and management. Daily capacity was estimated at up to thirty-five thousand board feet of lumber. In 1921, another major fire occurred, but the company was insufficiently insured for the damage and was unable to recover. Decades later, major tracts of the Town Creek holdings would become industrial forests under Georgia Pacific and International Paper. It is unknown whether traces of the Town Creek operation have ever been sought or found. (Wilmington Morning Star, September 25, 1914, and various dates thereafter)

Late in 1907, the first ceremonial spike was driven home by the son of Z.W. Whitehead, the principal local activist behind the railroad. Unfortunately, this event occurred during a series of financial crises affecting banks and trust companies, and the hope for capital support dried up before the work was barely begun. Construction slowed to nearly a halt while the company's principals scrambled to protect their project, eventually getting underway again in the summer of 1908.

A call for eighty thousand crossties in 1908 suggests the re-initiation of construction, an amount that would support about thirty miles of relatively lightweight 56-pound-per-yard rail. (It must have never been anticipated that trains would run very fast, perhaps reflecting the terrain and soil structure

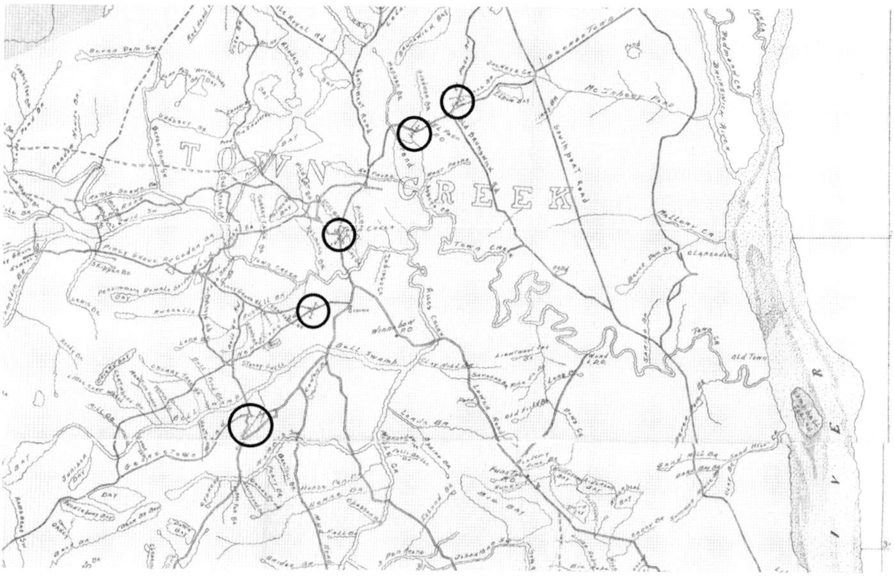

This map shows likely remnants of the defunct Carolina, Tennessee & Ohio Railroad some years earlier. Preexisting timber railroad bridges were in place at the circled locations at El Paso Road (near today's Lanvale Road), near El Paso itself, Town Creek, New Hope Road and in the Bell Swamp area just north of Bolivia. These would soon be connected to establish the WB&S route from Navassa to Bolivia, where it turned southeast to Southport. *Charles Henry Smith, "Map of Brunswick County N.C.," detail, 1910. State Archives of North Carolina.*

over which they were to run. Standard rail weights on interstate trunk lines would easily have been 75 to 120 pounds.) For nearly all of the route, the track was ballasted simply by the handy and readily available mix of packed sand and clay. This would have been scooped out from the sides of the railpath to build up a raised bed. Stone, a far more durable material, would have to wait until operations could support the expense.

The next year, progress was slowed down again by a significant lawsuit against the WB&S, as reported in the *Wilmington Morning Star* of November 20, 1909. The plaintiffs had apparently put $1,000 down on a misunderstood deal to purchase everything the railroad owned: rights-of-way, county-issued bonds, railroad iron, crossties, tools, mules, wagons and other vehicles, locomotive, steam-powered logging equipment, rolling stock, structures and all timber and real estate. The plaintiffs lost the case, but there were other minor suits naming the companies as defendants; for the most part, these others dealt with property issues.

Between the already-made pieces of the route (creek crossings and some of the Town Creek lumber area) lay stretches of virgin forest. In the age before mechanized equipment, the railroad's right-of-way had to be laboriously cleared with hand tools, mules and wagons, and progress was slow. For the next two years, the railway very gradually took shape, striking a line down toward Bolivia. There don't seem to be any records of the progress made or number of workers, but these first seventeen miles were not speedy, working out to a mere three-quarters of a mile per month.

An even larger challenge lay in determining the route beyond Bolivia (which had some signs of a small boomtown in anticipation of the coming railroad) and a further logical endpoint. Southport was obviously a strong and long-standing choice, with its deep-water mooring, earlier efforts to develop its waterfront and a couple of miles of previously graded right-of-way (recall William Weeks, who began volunteer grading for the South Atlantic & Northwestern in the 1890s). However, a path beyond Bolivia to Supply and Shallotte and into South Carolina was another possibility (and permission had indeed been given for this route), where connections could be made with trunk lines to Charleston, South Carolina, and other inland destinations.

Being nearer, Southport ultimately was chosen as the terminus, but it lay on the other side of exceptionally difficult terrain. The WB&S was faced with the formidable challenge of the unsurveyed, unsettled and never penetrated terrain beyond Bolivia. Here were to be found unsound ground, interlaced pools and bogs, primeval tangles of vines and deadfalls and innumerable swarms of insect pests—interspersed with basins of peaty silt and mucky soil types, just to add to the unattractiveness. Entirely unsuited to agriculture, the land had wild growth of gums, cypress, swamp oak, maple and scrub pine.

Setting aside the difficulty and expense of a straight-line route between Bolivia and Southport, one choice was in a southern approach, running the road toward Supply and then to Southport. This would parallel the Southport–Supply Road (now North Carolina Highway 211). The other approach was a northern bypass, skirting above the problem area and arriving at Southport from that direction.

The northern approach to Southport won out and yielded a path about six miles less (therefore less expensive) than the southern alternative and surveyed on solid enough footing to presumably support traffic. The route was able to work its way between the headwaters of Allen Creek and Orton Creek to the north and the truly wild terrain to the south, known locally as Half Hell as an indicator of its character. Today, this line is McKay Road southeast of Bolivia and Ridge Road along the southern edge of Boiling Springs Lake. This approach also allowed access to the hamlets of Goresville, Coolvale and Atwood approaching Southport.

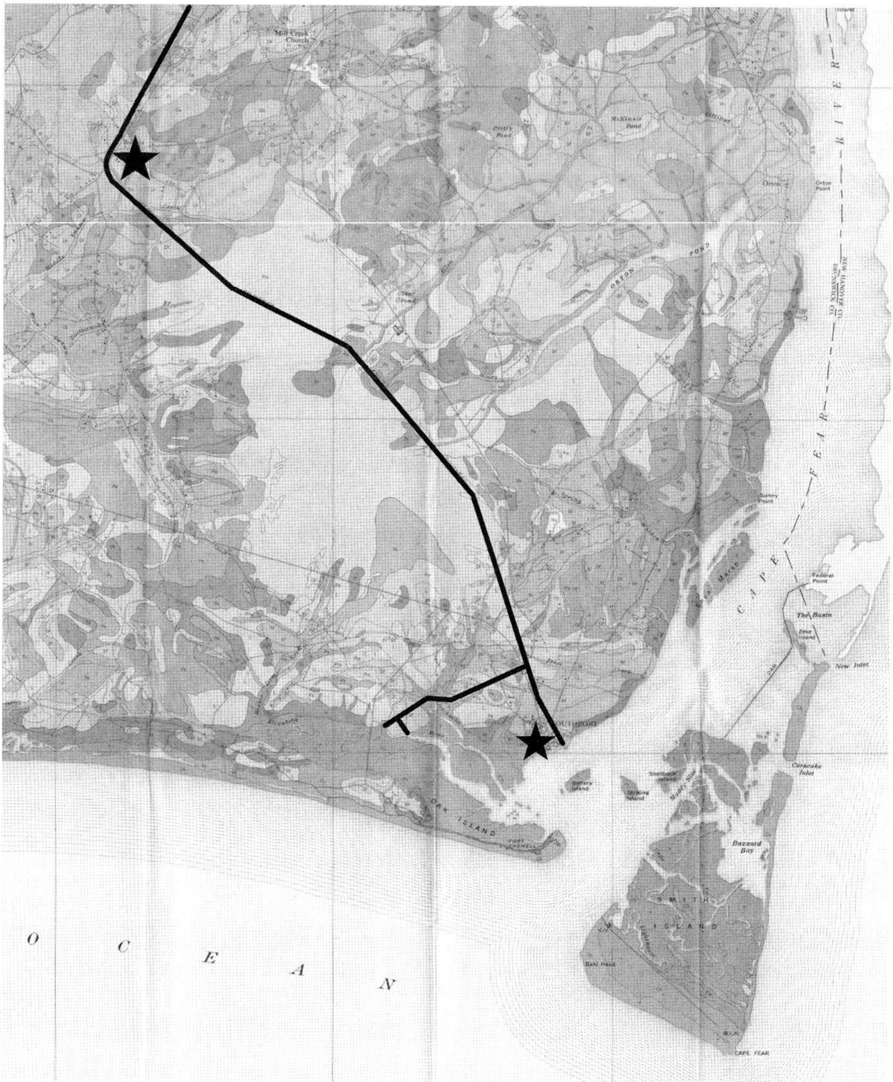

On this map, the blob (*lower center*) and surrounding light areas are mucky and unstable soil types, which the WB&S had to skirt in driving the line (*highlighted*) from Bolivia (*upper star*) left to Southport (*lower star*). *Soil Map of Brunswick County, detail, U.S. Department of Agriculture, 1932, digital.lib.ecu.edu.*

In 1910, principals of the WB&S bought out the interests of the Town Creek Railroad & Lumber Company. To capitalize this new start-up, $200,000 in stock was authorized for sale, with construction financed by stockholders and directors. In 1911, the railroad was authorized to sell bonds

The Town Creek Railroad & Lumber Company sold stock in 1906 to capitalize its development. Shown is a certificate for forty-five shares to A.J. McKinnon, who had business interests around Laurinburg, North Carolina. Signatures include Z.W. Whitehead (later president of the WB&S) and R.F. DeVane (perhaps an associate of McKinnon's from Red Springs). *Courtesy of Southport Historical Society.*

up to $300,000 for construction and equipment, borrowing to recapture the personal investment of the principals. Unlike earlier ventures, this time the company had real property and physical progress, and the bonds were backed by the value of all that property, with Wilmington Savings & Trust Company as the trustee. Southport itself was allowed to subscribe $15,000 for stock, subject to its provision that the railroad actually reached Southport by July 1, 1911.

Costs eventually came in at $240,000 for the thirty-mile line, remarkably inexpensive due to taking advantage of more than twenty-five years of work done by earlier ventures, not to mention extreme frugality in construction.

The company's principals were well aware of the productive capacity of the land, whether measured in forest products or cultivated crops. Traffic would be generated by fifteen to twenty logging and sawmill operators, turpentine processing and naval stores, shingles, cotton, truck produce (fruits

When the WB&S spun off from the Town Creek operation, it issued its own stock. Shown is a certificate for five shares to A.J. McKinnon, with officers noted as H.C. McQueen and M.J. Corbett, both Wilmington bankers. About twenty-five years later, Corbett would be named receiver for the company to settle its affairs. *Courtesy of Southport Historical Society.*

and vegetables), field crops, rice, peanuts and other root crops, processed fish and fish products, cattle and hogs and passenger service. Using the railroad interchange at Navassa near Wilmington, freight could proceed inland via Atlantic Coast Line or Seaboard Air Line or cross the river to Wilmington and points north.

As a short line, the WB&S was now relegated to being a mere feeder to the well-established Atlantic Coast Line and Seaboard Air Line. It became one of a host of so-called cracker barrel railroads, spread in great profusion and diversity throughout the country and serving narrow geographic interests and rural needs. Contemporaneous examples in North Carolina would have included the Durham & Southern (a forty-two-mile line built around tobacco interests), the Atlantic & North Carolina (hauling enough fish to be nicknamed the "Mullet Line") or the Laurinburg & Southern (a family-owned twenty-eight-mile line built primarily around commodity transportation). At the time, fifty of the fifty-eight railroads operating in the state could be classified as short lines, as defined in the *Annual Report* of the North Carolina Corporation Commission (1912).

The group of WB&S principals represents an interesting, if not entirely unexpected, mix of interests and concerns, tapping their respective strengths and professional affiliations. Of these, M.W. Divine may have been the most significant locally, with political, social, construction, banking, lumber and maritime activities—all of importance to the nascent railroad company. In varying degrees, they also would have been instrumental in subscribing capital through the WB&S offerings of bonds and stocks. The most significant linkages among them were in banking, forestry and construction materials.

With information from the North Carolina Newspaper Collection, Wilmington Directory 1911–12, Thirteenth Census of the United States, online compilations, obituaries and the *Wilmington Dispatch*, profiles of the principals include the following.

- Z.W. (Zollicofer Wiley) Whitehead: editor of the *Southern Lumber Journal*, manager of the *Carolina Fruit & Truckers Journal*, editor of the *Greensboro Patriot*, a director on several local bank boards, press associations and the North Carolina Pine Association. He was also editor of the *Fayetteville Observer* and secretary of the Fayetteville & Albemarle Railroad in the early 1890s, where he developed many contacts in foresting, farming and railroads. His young son would drive the ceremonial first spike to initiate construction in 1907, while he himself would drive the last spike in 1911 to conclude the project. His Wilmington home, built in 1899, still stands and is listed with the Historic Wilmington Foundation.

Z.W. Whitehead (1862–1923), one of the earliest principals and president of the WB&S. Wilmington Morning Star, *November 23, 1911.*

- R.F. DeVane: of Red Springs, had lumber and landholdings since the 1890s. In the early going, he and Whitehead were very active in securing timber deeds and right-of-way agreements. Later news items suggest that he apparently got in over his head in debt and was forced to sell land and other property in 1915 to settle claims. Later, he was named oil inspector for the North Carolina Board of Agriculture.

A.J. McKinnon (1862–1922), another of the earliest activists behind the WB&S. Wilmington Morning Star, *June 10, 1913.*

- Major A.J. McKinnon: operated large-scale farms (especially cotton) around Laurinburg and Maxton, vice president and treasurer of Southern Exchange Co. in Maxton, North Carolina (construction materials, poles, railroad ties, lumber and more), president of Maxton Alma & Southbound Railroad, candidate for commissioner of agriculture in 1916, activist in the Good Roads Association, a director of Lafayette Mutual Life Insurance Company, delegate to the Southern Cotton Congress in 1914.

- George H. Bellamy: state representative and senator from El Paso (around where Lanvale Road now runs), enduringly involved in county and state political activity. Occasionally nicknamed the "Duke of Brunswick," some of his other appointments included county superintendent of public education, tax commissioner and U.S. marshal. The 1910 census lists him as a farmer, landowner and a backer of the Town Creek Railroad & Lumber Company.

- Jackson Stanland: an original principal in the Town Creek and WB&S enterprise. Unfortunately, as Brunswick County sheriff, he was shot and killed while serving an arrest warrant in 1908.

- W.H. Chadbourn: president of Chadbourn Lumber Company, president and director of Citizens Building & Loan, president of Oakdale Cemetery Association, president of Wilmington, Chadbourn & Conway Railroad (despite the name, the road only ran between Conway, South Carolina, and Chadbourn, North Carolina, from 1885 to 1895), director of Wilmington Seacoast Railroad.

- M.J. Corbett: a director of Murchison National Bank, vice president of People's Savings Bank, president of the Corbett Company (dealer in provisions and a commission merchant, warehouse at Nutt and Brunswick Streets), president of Ocean Fisheries Company, president of Wilmington Chamber of Commerce. (Unknown to him, he would preside over the company's demise twenty-five years later.)

- H.C. (Henry Clay) McQueen: president and director of Murchison National Bank, president and director of People's Savings Bank, vice president and director of the Carolina Insurance Company, vice president of Wilmington Homestead & Loan Association.

- M. (Morrison) W. Divine: Son of Atlantic Coast Line Railroad general superintendent John Divine, New Hanover County commissioner, president of M.W. Divine & Company (dealer in paints, oils, roofing, glass, builders hardware and more), a director of Murchison National Bank, a director of People's Savings Bank, president of Chadbourn Lumber Company (on Wrightsville Sound), secretary/treasurer of Ocean Fisheries Company, a director of Oakdale Cemetery Association, on the executive committee of North Carolina Waterways Association.

- Herbert E. Goodwin: WB&S traffic manager.

The company took advantage of earlier work in and around Southport, where franchises were reassigned, rights of way defined and a route re-cleared and graded. Through 1911, newspapers published frequent excited updates about the progress of construction, which increasingly looked to be the "real deal." Surveying, clearing, grading, setting crossties, track laying and ballasting were reported as being underway on the last leg of the road between Bolivia and Southport. By the end of January, it was reported that the difficult swamp terrain was slowly being conquered as the roadbed penetrated into virgin territory below Bolivia. In April, grading had been completed as far as Goresville (today near the southern end of the Boiling Spring Lakes impoundment). The terrain was challenging, allowing track to be laid at a modest half mile a day. In June, with a deadline looming, a force of one hundred men was hastily recruited to work two shifts a day to accelerate progress. The line reached the city limits just one day before the expiration of its July 1 deadline, satisfying the performance demands of finance underwriters.

Of the above, Sheriff Jackson Stanland never got to see the finished road. While serving an arrest warrant for breaking and entering in 1908, he was shot and killed. As widely reported in newspapers, the assailant, one Jesse Walker, was apprehended and held in the jail in Southport to await trial. After a few weeks, he escaped and somehow made his way to Oklahoma, where he eventually was arrested for another slaying. Oklahoma authorities returned him to North Carolina to complete his original sentence, but he escaped from the local jail again in 1914 and hid out in the Wilmington area. Walker was recaptured early in 1915 and was sentenced to thirty years in the state penitentiary but escaped in 1919. He fled to Gulfport, Mississippi, where he apparently reformed and lived a stable life of respectability. It seems he carried a guilty conscience, however, and came back to Raleigh in 1935 to turn himself in to finish his sentence. Authorities there decided to parole him but then sent him back to Oklahoma to complete his sentence in that state. Curiously, the Oklahoma authorities also paroled him, and he went on his way. Granted, the story has little to do with railroads (except perhaps how Walker got from state to state), but his earlier exploits and later reappearance made major headlines in area newspapers in the 1930s. Sheriff Stanland's name was inscribed on the North Carolina Peace Officers Memorial in 1908. (Movies have been made with less of a premise than this.)

The editor of the *Southern Pines Tourist* magazine (July 1911) waxed positively euphoric in an editorial praising Southport. In part, his comments beamed out some bright prospects and braggadocio for the enterprising town:

> *Southport's more enthusiastic boomers feel sure that Southport will some day practically wipe Wilmington off the map. They can see no future for the Cape Fear City, which has long been North Carolina's chief seaport, and they expect to cut a much bigger figure, as a shipping port, than Wilmington, in all its proud career, ever cut.*

Later in July, a ceremonial last spike was driven by Z.W. Whitehead, the company's president, a kind of bookend to the first-spike event where his

Likely taken in 1911, this is the only known photo of the WB&S during construction, in a view along a cleared path through the woods. Some were known as "Russians," who were camped at Clear Pond, now known as Spring Lake in the Boiling Spring Lakes community. Note the ties being ballasted by packed sand, a cheap and quick method but ultimately unsuitable. *From the collection of Mildred Mercer, courtesy of the* Brunswick Beacon, *November 13, 1986.*

son did the honors. In August, the WB&S finally ran the first train over its tracks with twelve freight cars to test its construction, make adjustments and begin its revenue service—eagerly sought now that the upfront money had been spent on construction. Several newly built lumber enterprises along the way promised additional freight income, and land was being cleared and developed all along the route.

The *Wilmington Morning Star* (October 1, 1911) trumpeted praises for the untapped potential of Brunswick County as the WB&S began operations. Noting the absence of meaningful transportation through the central undeveloped part of the county, the railroad was expected to prosper from the abundance of virgin timber and the fertility of the soil for a wide variety of truck produce and access to markets for field crops like corn, produce and peanuts. All of this would be in addition to the persistently lingering aim of year-round coal operations in Southport so that the railroad would

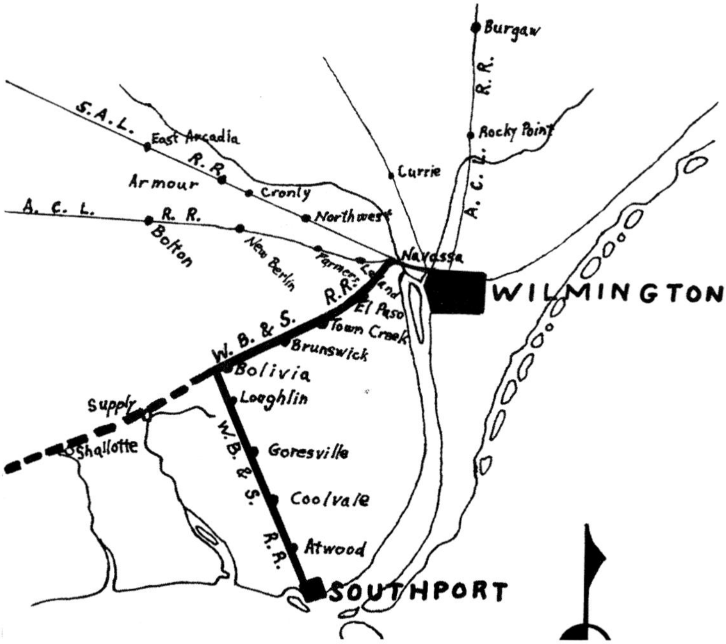

The first published map of the WB&S (detail). Evidently hand-drawn and not to scale, it shows the approximate route (*solid line*) and a potential extension beyond Supply (*dashed line*). The leg from Bolivia to Southport actually arced a bit to the north to avoid unsolid ground. *Redrawn by author from source image,* Wilmington Morning Star, *October 1, 1911.*

be "destined to play no small part in the development of eastern North Carolina…at the same time make a city of world-wide importance of Southport as one of the South Atlantic gateways to be reckoned with in the future."

For a thirty-mile short line, the sights were set high indeed!

Chapter 7

LET'S HAVE A PARTY

Toward the end of 1911, the Wilmington, Brunswick & Southern Railroad was ready to join scores of other railroads operating in the state. After four years, the entire thirty-mile length of track was deemed ready for full service, and a grand opening festival was planned for November 23 in Southport. Civic groups and churches were all excitedly enlisted to plan for and support the effort. The local chamber of commerce even had a special notice printed conspicuously on the front page of the *Southport News*, inviting one and all to the great celebration—including the no-fail incentive of free food. A companion notice (caps and all) in the *Wilmington Morning Star* of November 20 gave an "All Aboard" call and encouraged one and all to

> *take a day off and ride through the vast domains of undeveloped country laying at our back doors and which is destined to early become the trucking paradise of the Old North State. Patriotic Speeches by Statesmen and Orators, Boat Races and Parades, Grand Display of Battleships, Foot Races, Base Ball, Military Drills, Free Dinner and an Old Fashioned Barbecue of Beef, Pork, Mutton, Venison, Possum, Etc., including All of the Good Things Grown and Produced in Brunswick County.*
>
> *A Good Time Guaranteed Everybody and Perfect Order Insured!*

The evening *Wilmington Dispatch* recapped the day's festivities under a large front-page headline of "Southport Gloriously Celebrating Today."

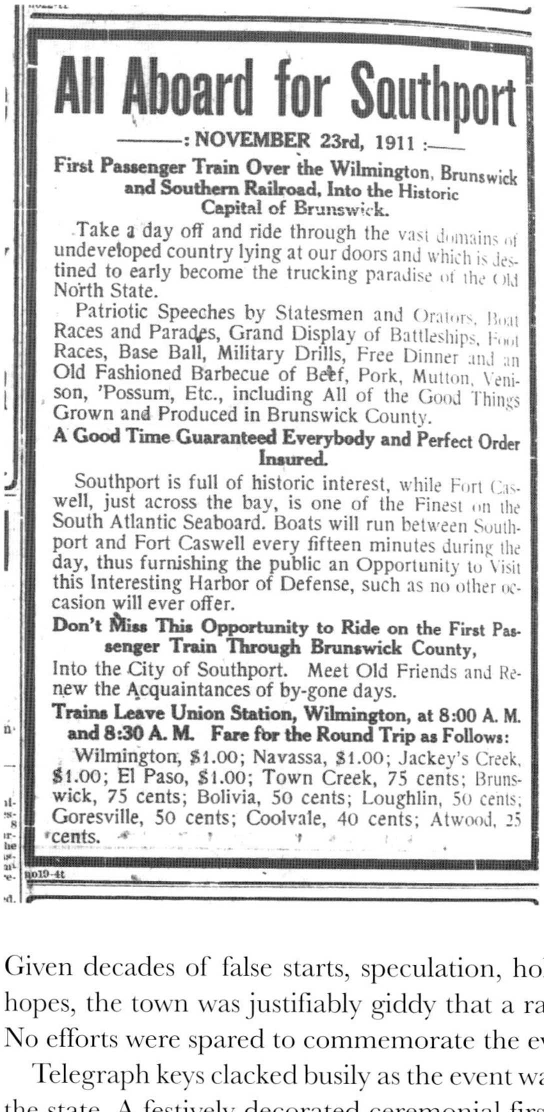

All Aboard for Southport

——: NOVEMBER 23rd, 1911 :——

First Passenger Train Over the Wilmington, Brunswick and Southern Railroad, Into the Historic Capital of Brunswick.

Take a day off and ride through the vast domains of undeveloped country lying at our doors and which is destined to early become the trucking paradise of the Old North State.

Patriotic Speeches by Statesmen and Orators, Boat Races and Parades, Grand Display of Battleships, Foot Races, Base Ball, Military Drills, Free Dinner and an Old Fashioned Barbecue of Beef, Pork, Mutton, Venison, 'Possum, Etc., including All of the Good Things Grown and Produced in Brunswick County.

A Good Time Guaranteed Everybody and Perfect Order Insured.

Southport is full of historic interest, while Fort Caswell, just across the bay, is one of the Finest on the South Atlantic Seaboard. Boats will run between Southport and Fort Caswell every fifteen minutes during the day, thus furnishing the public an Opportunity to Visit this Interesting Harbor of Defense, such as no other occasion will ever offer.

Don't Miss This Opportunity to Ride on the First Passenger Train Through Brunswick County,

Into the City of Southport. Meet Old Friends and Renew the Acquaintances of by-gone days.

Trains Leave Union Station, Wilmington, at 8:00 A. M. and 8:30 A. M. Fare for the Round Trip as Follows:

Wilmington, $1.00; Navassa, $1.00; Jackey's Creek, $1.00; El Paso, $1.00; Town Creek, 75 cents; Brunswick, 75 cents; Bolivia, 50 cents; Loughlin, 50 cents; Goresville, 50 cents; Coolvale, 40 cents; Atwood, 25 cents.

no19-4t

Announcement about the dedication festivities for the WB&S. The special round-trip fare of one dollar was about a half day's pay at the time. Wilmington Morning Star, *November 22, 1911.*

Given decades of false starts, speculation, hollow promises and unfulfilled hopes, the town was justifiably giddy that a railroad was finally completed. No efforts were spared to commemorate the event.

Telegraph keys clacked busily as the event was widely reported throughout the state. A festively decorated ceremonial first train behind Atlantic Coast Line locomotive No. 456 departed from Wilmington about 8:30 a.m. Behind it were five coaches with elected dignitaries, railroad officials and a special chartered car with a reunion group of about one hundred former Southport men, the "back home boys," each with a commemorative badge and "jolly as a lark," according to dispatches. Along the way, stops at the mid-county settlements of Town Creek and Winnabow allowed more to board. This first train pulled in to Southport after a trip of about two and a half hours and was welcomed by cheers from the thousands already assembled there.

Atlantic Coast Line locomotive #454, a sibling to #456, which pulled celebrants to Southport for festivities in 1911. *Courtesy of Wilmington Railroad Museum, Wilmington, North Carolina.*

A second train arrived shortly after, with more celebrants. Besides the railroad principals, special guests included the governor, a U.S. senator and representative, mayors from nearby cities and towns, a state senator and prominent local leaders. All told, about five hundred people jammed the two trains on the inaugural trip to Southport for dedication ceremonies, an excursion special enough to command one-dollar round-trip tickets from Wilmington. A troop of mounted marshals and an honor guard of veterans of the Spanish-American War were on hand to escort the dignitaries to the speakers' platform, accompanied by a military band.

Captain John Harper's venerable steamer *Wilmington* was packed to the gunwales with a crowd of five hundred passengers who also came downriver to join the celebration. The revenue cutter *Seminole* also arrived, along with a flotilla of other watercraft and the torpedo boats *McDonough* and *DeLong*. More people streamed in from down-county communities and country settlements. This brought the estimated total of celebrants to five thousand, more than tripling Southport's population at the time. Proportionally, this was the "biggest deal" ever experienced there, and town pride justifiably swelled with having finally accomplished something important. The *Charlotte Observer* wryly noted that pickpockets also had a good day, according to the sheriff, "touching" more than one hundred people for cash, papers, jewelry and watches.

Captain John Harper's durable steamer *Wilmington*, which made trips for many years (1891–1917) between Wilmington and Southport. For the WB&S dedication, the vessel was packed with about five hundred passengers. State Port Pilot, *"The Way It Was" series.*

The venerable live oaks of Franklin Park had never witnessed such a gathering. On the long speakers' stand, the band members found their seats to one side and continued to play while the dignitaries engaged in customary rounds of hand-shaking, finding seats and generally settling in. Beneath a floral arch, a speakers' stand was flanked by American flags, and the crowd thronged near to hear the celebratory speeches. As reported in the *Wilmington Morning Star* of November 24, community booster and attorney Robert W. Davis of Southport at last began the festivities with a folksy welcoming address, claiming that "every patriotic North Carolinian is filled with righteous pride and devotion and loyalty to [this] seaport city."

Then, in the customary florid and superlative oratory of the times, he exhorted the crowd to "see and know that nature has destined Southport to be the greatest seaport on the eastern coast…be glad that the dream of Southport's railroad is real, and is the initiative step to make North Carolina [the] leading competitor with Pennsylvania and Ohio for all our mountains with coal and minerals."

In a real test for attendees, this was followed by at least nine more speeches, including congratulations from Governor William W. Kitchin and an hour-long oration by U.S. senator F.M. Simmons. Much was made about the line having been built very inexpensively for only $200,000. This likely reflects being able to cheaply acquire twenty or more years' worth of work from the many earlier false starts, along with the frugality typical of initial railroad construction. Finally, Z.W. Whitehead, the president of the road, was presented with a gold cane by appreciative citizens who recognized his tenacious advocacy of the enterprise.

At long last, the huge and hungry crowd joined in at the promised hearty barbecue feast among the trees in Franklin Park, prepared by the ladies of Southport churches and social groups (perhaps with some biblical tongue-in-cheek references to "feeding the five thousand"). To add to the hometown flavor of the event, menu items were all supposed to be from Brunswick County. As such, the selections were heavy on seafood, wild game and pork, with an assortment of beans and greens. Although a bounty was offered for successfully hunting down a bear, it was ruefully noted that the affair lacked that particular delicacy (the bears apparently had the good sense to hide out in the wilds until the ruckus had passed).

The crowd then dispersed for an afternoon of scheduled recreational and processional activities, which included a lively water parade of motorboats and steamers, energetic sports and field events and military unit reviews. Shuttle boats left frequently for the mile-and-a-half trip to Fort Caswell for tours and demonstrations of small arms and drill maneuvers. The special guests and invitees on the speakers' platform took a seven-mile cruise on

Dedication day for the WB&S, a festive occasion all around with speeches, military demonstrations, music, barbecues, water exhibitions and more. An estimated five thousand people showed up for the day, brought in by special trains, river steamers and other craft, automobiles and wagons. State Port Pilot, *"The Way It Was" series.*

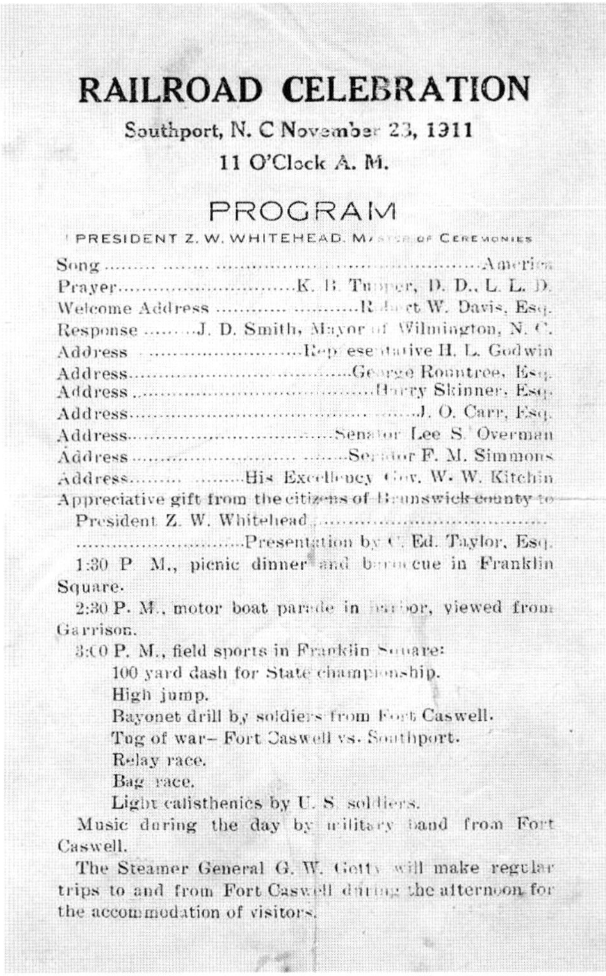

RAILROAD CELEBRATION

Southport, N. C November 23, 1911

11 O'Clock A. M.

PROGRAM

PRESIDENT Z. W. WHITEHEAD, MASTER OF CEREMONIES

Song ....America

Prayer ....K. B. Tupper, D. D., L. L. D.

Welcome Address ....Robert W. Davis, Esq.

Response ....J. D. Smith, Mayor of Wilmington, N. C.

Address ....Representative H. L. Godwin

Address ....George Rountree, Esq.

Address ....Harry Skinner, Esq.

Address ....J. O. Carr, Esq.

Address ....Senator Lee S. Overman

Address ....Senator F. M. Simmons

Address ....His Excellency Gov. W. W. Kitchin

Appreciative gift from the citizens of Brunswick county to President Z. W. Whitehead ....Presentation by C. Ed. Taylor, Esq.

1:30 P. M., picnic dinner and barbecue in Franklin Square.

2:30 P. M., motor boat parade in harbor, viewed from Garrison.

3:00 P. M., field sports in Franklin Square:

100 yard dash for State championship.
High jump.
Bayonet drill by soldiers from Fort Caswell.
Tug of war– Fort Caswell vs. Southport.
Relay race.
Bag race.
Light calisthenics by U. S. soldiers.

Music during the day by military band from Fort Caswell.

The Steamer General G. W. Getty will make regular trips to and from Fort Caswell during the afternoon for the accommodation of visitors.

The dedication program for the Wilmington, Brunswick & Southern Railroad. Patriotic sentiments were always strong, in this case with the song "America." There wouldn't be an official national anthem until 1931, when "The Star-Spangled Banner" was so designated. *Courtesy of Southport Historical Society.*

the revenue cutter *Seminole*, allegedly testing and sounding the depths of the Cape Fear shipping channel. Eventually, they gathered for a banquet at the quarantine station, served under the direction of the station's chef, with many rounds of toasts and applause. In December, the *Southport News* published a special souvenir supplement commemorating the occasion. (Alas, there seem to be no surviving examples of this supplement. It would undoubtedly shed more light on the scope of the festivities.)

The event even spawned a couple of poetic odes, including one by Kate Stuart, a lifelong Southport fixture and longtime operator of a popular waterfront boardinghouse/hotel in Southport. Miss Kate, as she was familiarly known, apparently thought she had not been properly invited to the grand party. Legend has it that she somehow requisitioned a handcar and pumped her way in on the rails to make her entrance to the festivities. Given that she was sixty-seven years old at the time, this would have been quite a feat. Her entire commemorative poem (loaded with local references):

On old Rhett Street each one you meet
Just shakes hands all around;
For don't you see, they say with glee,
The railroad's come to town.

From far Supply to Calabash,
See how they cover ground.
They've come to help us celebrate,
The railroad's come to town.

Good farmer Pyke, just from the "Pole,"
Who often used to frown,
Now wears a vest, substantial smile,
The railroad's come to town.

Bring out your flags, let us all hurrah!
An do the thing up brown.
It has been coming forty years,
By Jinks, it's got to town!

Another one, offered by someone with the initials S.A.M., offers this assessment of the day's expectations. It was penned a couple of months later in 1912 under the title "In Dear Old Southport." The author found some humor in playing on the incidental pickpocketing and pilfering that went on during the grand opening event, not to mention a rather condescending point of view:

Strange things are happening every day, but the strangest of all, so it seems,
Is the way in which Wilmington people were "touched" when Southport awoke from her dreams.

We all know the story of this dear little Burg that never knew sorrow nor tears;
But like dear old Rip Van Winkle of old, just slept and slept for years.

Now this is no fable, nor is it a joke. Wilmington people were "touched" when Southport awoke.
The story is simple; it happened this way, in dear old Southport on Railroad Day.

The day broke glorious, grand, and great, just such a day to celebrate.
The city folks and the "back home boys" decided to go and share the joys
Of the simple little village folk, who had slept so long, but had not awoke.

Two very fat men who were awful wise, they'd been used to working the "city guys,"
Had read the papers, saw at a glance, that this was the time when they'd have a chance

To do as the railroad, "make a haul," and "touch" the people both great and small.
And from all accounts they did succeed, for money and diamonds they had a greed.

Now the point of this story, strange to say, 'twas the city folks "touched" and not the "jay."
They took a day off to have a lark, but proved to be an easy mark.

Almost immediately, freight service was initiated. Revenue was urgently needed to offset the hundreds of thousands of dollars already sunk into timber rights and construction. A few months later, the WB&S was purchased outright by a syndicate of some of the earlier principals, among them M.J. Corbett, A.J. McKinnon, H.C. McQueen and John F. McNair.

By February 1912, a turning wye was built near where Leonard Street bends today, just beyond a subdivision attractively named Swamp Gardens and the headwaters of Bonnet Creek. This convenience provided the means of turning trains around and repositioning an engine to the head end of a train. As regularly scheduled passenger service began, it was boasted that the thirty-mile trip took under two hours. Today, we would view this average speed of about fifteen miles per hour with disdain. However, it was an immense improvement over the main alternative of river steamers, whose four-hour service was at least partially dependent on tides and weather. And it would have been vastly better than a trip by automobile of up to six hours, contending with the primitive roads of the time.

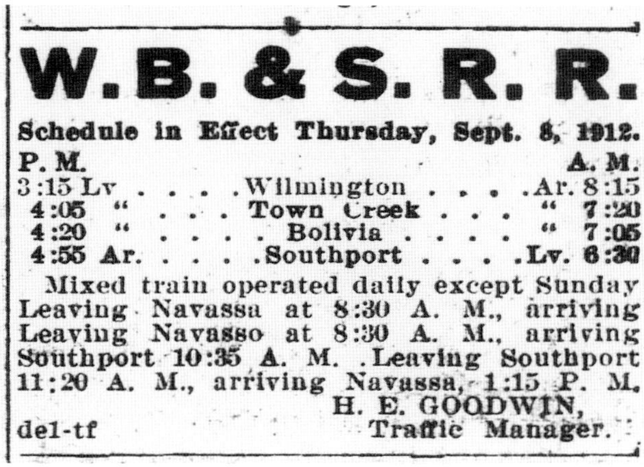

W. B. & S. R. R.

Schedule in Effect Thursday, Sept. 5, 1912.

P. M.			A. M.
3:15 Lv	Wilmington	Ar.	8:15
4:05 "	Town Creek	"	7:20
4:20 "	Bolivia	"	7:05
4:55 Ar.	Southport	Lv.	6:30

Mixed train operated daily except Sunday Leaving Navassa at 8:30 A. M., arriving Leaving Navasso at 8:30 A. M., arriving Southport 10:35 A. M. Leaving Southport 11:20 A. M., arriving Navassa, 1:15 P. M.

H. E. GOODWIN,
Traffic Manager.

del-tf

The first published schedule of the WB&S, just after passenger service was formally begun. Only two intermediate stops were listed between Wilmington and Southport; more would be added as business grew along the line. Wilmington Morning Star, *December 1, 1912.*

By July 1912, passenger service was officially inaugurated out of the handsome new Southport station, which included such refinements as electricity and telephone service and the later addition of express package service and telegraph. One-way trips cost seventy-five cents, based on a rate of two and a half cents per mile as established by the North Carolina Corporation Commission. Rural stations like that at "Brunswick" (between Winnabow and Bolivia) were quite the opposite of the Southport facility—rough board-and-batten construction with a metal roof, rarely electrified, a bare minimum number of windows and maybe a stove for heat. This was described by Landmark Preservation Associates in *Comprehensive Historical/Architectural Site Survey of Brunswick County North Carolina* (2010):

> *The* [station] *erected in the sparsely populated Bell Swamp section is a rough, warehouse-like building of board-and-batten frame construction with a metal-sheathed front-gable roof….The east elevation door is constructed of z-braced battens, as are the shutters of the side windows, which do not have window sashes, and may not have had them originally. The west elevation appears to have been the front through which passengers entered the building. Its 2/2 windows with z-braced shutters are the only original glazed windows in the building. The unfinished interior was warmed by two stoves, served by tile block flues that are supported at the level of the ceiling joists by strap iron hangers. The lack of interior wall and ceiling sheathing reveals the construction, which is intermediate between conventional stud construction and boxed construction….* [Its] *simplicity suggests its freight function was primary.*

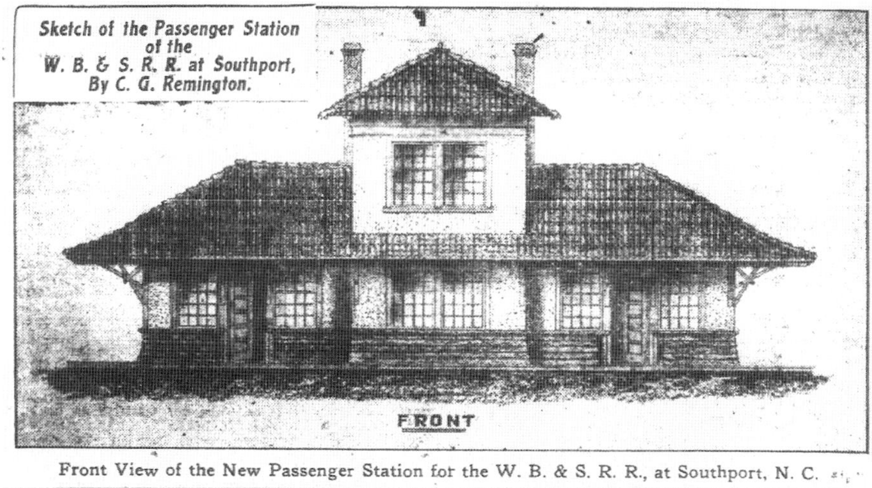

Concept drawing for the Southport station of the Wilmington, Brunswick & Southern Railroad. The station would be completed the following May. Wilmington Morning Star, *October 1, 1911.*

Southport train station, popular postcard image. In 1913, the station had to be shifted from its original spot and rotated to more conveniently align with the frontage tracks. It also allowed pedestrians to access the station without having to cross the tracks. *Durwood Barbour Collection of North Carolina Postcards (P077), North Carolina Collection Photographic Archives, Wilson Library, UNC–Chapel Hill. Courtesy of the North Carolina Department of Natural and Cultural Resources.*

Left: W.W. Kitchin (1827–1912), governor of North Carolina and speaker when the WB&S was dedicated. His term was marked by infrastructure improvements and bank stabilization. *Library of Congress.*

Right: U.S. senator F.M. Simmons (1854–1940), a powerful politician who served for thirty years and ran the Democratic political machine in North Carolina. *Library of Congress.*

U.S. representative Hannibal L. Godwin (1873–1929), a seven-term Democratic congressman whose interests ran to river and harbor improvements and swamp reclamation. He had just been reelected to his third term in office when he agreed to help celebrate the completion of the WB&S. *Library of Congress.*

For the first year, the WB&S office was in the building at the left side of this postcard image next to the old U.S. Custom House. When that block was demolished to build the new custom house, the WB&S moved its office to 23 Market Street at the business of one of its early investors, M.W. Divine (circular sign in the center). In the 1920s, the WB&S moved its manager back to Southport. *Courtesy of New Hanover County Public Library, North Carolina Room, View of Wilmington, N.C., A 12241. Wilmington Harbor Collection, New Hanover County Public Library Digital Archives (oclc.org).*

The WB&S also saw a need to establish a presence in Wilmington, and in 1912, it found some space to operate an agency for passenger tickets and small freight shipments. The Wilmington City Directory listed the railroad for the first time in 1913, operating at an unnumbered location next to the old U.S. Custom House at the foot of Princess Street.

By Jinks, it's got to town!

Chapter 8

LET THE OPERATIONS BEGIN

When the WB&S began operations, Southport, Bolivia and Shallotte were the only incorporated towns in Brunswick County. Bolivia, just incorporated in 1911, lay along the old Wilmington-Georgetown Road (later Ocean Highway or U.S. Highway 17). Already a settlement at the junction of surface roads, it saw itself as an inland center for forest products, sawn lumber, shingles, tobacco, naval stores and other agricultural products to move to market. By some calculations, it was also a potential point for future tracks to branch off to Shallotte and Little River, South Carolina. Likely fueled by these speculative prospects, by 1915 the town had a post office, stores, sawmills, churches and a hotel, and it was aiming to become the new county seat.

Having recovered from its fit of festive excess, Southport returned to normal, and the WB&S settled in to the rhythms of humdrum workaday activity, running unglamorous little trains back and forth through its thirty-mile domain. The new station was a welcome addition to Southport's growing commercial district, although the station had to be moved to better accommodate trains and to lay in additional tracks. The accompanying loss of six ancient live oak trees much prized by the locals was regretted, and the company offered its apologies to the city.

An increasing number of sawmills and farms around Bolivia and near the route provided the necessary cargo to help sustain its operations. A major coal operation never developed in Southport, but small-scale coal shipments were trundled down from Wilmington to serve local demand

The strategic inland location of Bolivia led to several years of effort to move the county seat there. One proposal even suggested subdividing Brunswick County so Southport could retain its status, albeit of a smaller county. Those efforts (and vigorous opposition from Southport) eventually failed in Bolivia's bid to become the county seat in 1920, and much of the town's progress disappeared as well. The 1920 U.S. census listed its population as just 199. It wouldn't be until more than fifty years later that the town was finally approved to be the new county seat. By that time, of course, the railroad was long gone. Rather than establish in built-up Bolivia itself, the county developed vacant acreage about a mile south of town.

and to refuel ships that came to call. (Curiously, none of the WB&S locomotives was fired by coal.) Recently built fish-processing facilities (shoreline and floating) employed hundreds of people to prepare and pack shrimp, oysters and marketable fish. Tons of menhaden and bycatch fish provided oil, meal and byproducts for fertilizer. In a few years, the railroad would obtain the franchise for postal service, replacing the river steamer that had carried the mail for many years.

In 1913, the railroad acquired a parcel of about 165 feet of waterfront and quickly built a T-shaped pier 340 feet out into the river with a 400-foot wharf. Besides these shoreline facilities, passenger service was also healthy, and the company was boasting of running two or three passenger coaches on daily trips to Wilmington. With only one locomotive and a single track, more often than not these would be mixed consist trains, a combination of the passenger coaches with whatever was being transported in freight cars.

In 1914, the company built a fifty-thousand-gallon water tank for its locomotives and for the coaling operations and ships. That same year, Western Union telegraph service was moved from the Southern Bell Telephone building in Southport to the new station, with lines to Wilmington strung along the railroad's right-of-way. The company also negotiated with the U.S. government to build a twelve-mile spur starting in Atwood, about where Highways 211 and 87 meet today. From there, the spur ran to the southwest, crossing Dutchman Creek and ending up at Barnes Bluff, a bit to the west of today's South Harbor Village Marina. This was potentially a benefit to Fort Caswell, but that was a short-lived promise; it never reached the fort itself, for after World War I, the fort would be well on its way to its decommissioning in 1920. However, other enterprises were

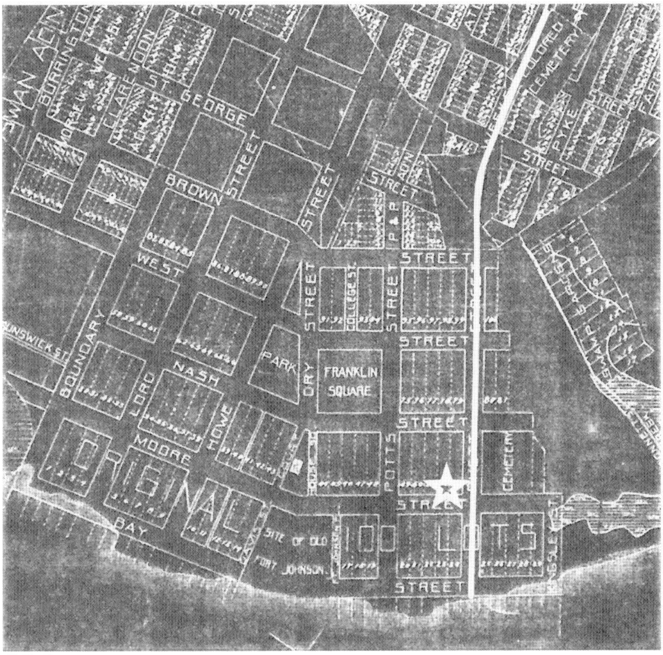

The lower end of the WB&S in Southport (*solid line on Rhett Street, right of center*). The station is noted with a star. The town had now grown considerably beyond the 1891 expansion, as shown in chapter 3. *"Plat Survey of Southport," detail, M. Fargusson, 1915. Courtesy of Southport Historical Society.*

established nearby, suggested by today's Fish Factory Road on that side of the creek. Offices also were established in Wilmington, in a building adjacent to the custom house along the river.

Motive power for the WB&S was initially provided by a holdover wood-burner locomotive of unknown provenance from the Town Creek Lumber acquisition. In 1915, the company purchased a secondhand wood-burner engine and five boxcars from the Georgia Car & Locomotive Company of Atlanta. Although this second locomotive saw service for only three years, it was a great help as the company coped with increasing traffic, both freight and passenger. The company's assessed value was $80,534, which strikes one as really low. By contrast, according to the *North Carolina Yearbook* from the *Raleigh News & Observer* (1915), the Atlantic Coast Line and Seaboard Air Line Railroads, which together had about the same number of miles of track in Brunswick County as the WB&S, had a combined assessed valuation in the county of nearly $800,000.

The year 1915 also saw the WB&S claim much growth in passenger trips. Some of that traffic was generated by military personnel at nearby Fort Caswell. When baseball season came around, teams and fans from the fort would travel up to Wilmington in lively competition with the local talent, including the team from the Atlantic Coast Line Railroad. Competition

Information from www.msrailroads.com suggests that the company's second locomotive (4-4-0 configuration) ran through quite a number of owners. It was built in 1889 by the Rhode Island Locomotive Works. Before the WB&S, the locomotive served the Macon Construction Co. in Georgia, the Georgia Southern & Florida Railroad and the Macon & Birmingham Railroad. Then it was listed for sale at the Georgia Car & Locomotive Company in Atlanta. After only three years for the WB&S as #200 (1915–18), it was sold to the Southern Iron & Equipment Co. and finally to the Alabama, Florida & Gulf Railroad, where it ended its days sometime in the 1920s. The Rhode Island company itself was merged with several other locomotive works to become American Locomotive Co., or ALCO.

between Fort Caswell and Wilmington municipal leagues was a lively affair for several years, especially for baseball, when extra streetcars would be put into service to carry fans to the ball fields. During a time when local newspapers tended to sprinkle their sports copy with colorful phrases, even this notice in the *Wilmington Morning Star* of March 23, 1912, must have stood out as it hoped for fair weather for a baseball game:

> *Each husky athlete of the local clan, fit and fine after a hard week's work, retired last night hoping fervently that Phoebus Apollo* [allusion to the Greek god of light, or the sun] *may see fit to race into the eastern sky this morning with flaming chariot to bring a perfect day to Wilmington's sport loving population.*

For a couple of years, the WB&S shipped three hundred to five hundred carloads of holly for holiday markets up north. In a related development during this time, a burgeoning network of improved roads was gradually making point-to-point travel much easier. More on this portentous development will be found in the next chapter.

The company was apparently confident enough in its early years to sink some resources into other activities. Besides active freight shipments from Southport for fish processing and many lumber operations along its length, by 1916 it was also operating morning and evening passenger service between Southport and Wilmington. Timetables of the period show passenger departures from Southport at 6:45 a.m. and 6:20 p.m., with the intervening accommodation leaving at 3:45 p.m. Speed was never the railroad's strong suit; an anecdote of the time relates how a couple of soldiers were complaining about the pace of travel. Overhearing their

Top: A Rhode Island 4-4-0 locomotive of this design (1890) was put on sale by the Georgia Car & Locomotive Company and sold to the WB&S in 1915 as its locomotive #200. After three years, the WB&S sold it. *Photo from* Rhode Island Locomotive Works, *Edward J. Ozog.*

Bottom: In the mid-1910s, this group of ladies on an excursion pose near the railroad's first locomotive, parked on a side track in Southport. The woodpile serving as a "bench" was placed for handy refueling alongside the track. State Port Pilot, *"The Way It Was" series.*

conversation, a lady passenger gave them a mock reprimand, pointing out that they should respect God's creations, even those that creep, a sarcastic reference to the railroad.

The year 1916 also saw long-overdue improvements to the company's pier and deteriorating coal dock. The latter had been built about fifteen years earlier and was in dubious condition. Likely underbuilt to begin with, they were suffering the effects of river currents, floating debris and tides over the years.

To improve its access to the Wilmington waterfront (and perhaps to avoid interchange complications with the Atlantic Coast Line or Seaboard Air Line), the company also purchased eight acres of land on Eagle Island

In the early years, train arrivals in Southport were often a bit of an occasion, as shown here about 1914 (based on the locomotive). The WB&S had an old 4-4-0 wood burner in service, soon to get help from a similar engine for heavy demand at the time. State Port Pilot, *"The Way It Was" series.*

across from Dock Street. The parcel ran parallel to the causeway of the time, with about 220 feet of Cape Fear River frontage and about 1,600 feet depth. Just how this property would connect to WB&S track is unclear, although it is possible that a portion of an abandoned and far older railroad right-of-way (Wilmington & Manchester) across the island could have been repurposed. Also in this year, a brief rumor emerged that Seaboard Air Line Railroad was interested in acquiring the WB&S.

By 1917, the railroad had moved its Wilmington agency from its Princess Street location due to construction of a new U.S. Custom House building. Very conveniently, it made a short-distance hop to the opposite side of the block to 23 Market Street. This was the longtime location for M.W. Divine Co., dealing in paints, turpentine and building supplies. It also happened to be one of the businesses owned by its namesake, a sometime county commissioner, officer of the Cape Fear Club and a principal of the WB&S at its start.

For the company's duration, much of the dependable freight traffic consisted of loads of fishmeal, the making of which was a major part of Southport's industrial activity for that period. Local papers reported that in 1911, for instance, a floating factory came to Southport, capable of processing up to ten thousand barrels of fish a day. In 1914, the Southport Fish Scrap and Oil Company began operations, employing up to four hundred workers. In season, these and other companies received untold tons of menhaden, shad, mullet or byproducts of other catches and then ground and dried them and pressed them for fish oil, with the remains to be further processed for fertilizer or animal feed.

An extension of the line from Bolivia to Shallotte (and points beyond) had received permission in the early days of the railroad. Although it was further discussed in 1919, it was doubtful that there would be sufficient traffic to warrant the investment, and the proposal was rejected. The idea of a major coaling station was not quite dead yet, however, and Senator F.M. Simmons consulted with M.J. Corbett, one of the original WB&S principals, as he continued to try to make a case for such a facility to serve the U.S. Navy.

Cut lumber and forest products were another commodity that kept the short line active. In addition to forty thousand passenger trips reported for 1919 (its highwater mark), there were at least fourteen sawmills along the line that shipped all their product on the WB&S, and Brunswick County had fifteen turpentine stills in operation. Besides clearing out land for a couple of miles on either side of the rail line, logging and sawmill operations had a downside effect. Heavy exploitation led to deforestation of the native and primeval long-leaf pine species without much thought for replacement. Cleared tracts could be planted for agricultural products and truck produce, but making the transition from forest floor to crop agriculture was an iffy process. Clearing land was very labor intensive, and the soil's nutrient value for other crops required repeated treatments with fertilizer. Ultimately,

Processed fishmeal and pressed oil were loaded onto boxcars for the trip up to Navassa for final processing. During the hot days of summer, sometimes boys would hop on board for a free ride to points north, where they could join friends or just have an adventure out of town, perhaps all the way to the end of the line. Unfortunately, spending an hour or more in a hot boxcar with fishmeal tended to make these homegrown hobos smell like fishmeal, too. They soon found out that the cloying fragrance of such cargo did not endear them to anyone once they arrived. It was also a dead giveaway as to what they had been up to once they returned home. It was reported that the fish-processing industry itself was taken to task by the Wilmington city commissioners. An item in the *Wilmington Morning Star* of June 14, 1922, tells how plant operators were summoned upriver to hear complaints about the disagreeable odors wafting from their products when unloading in Navassa.

replacement crops could not fully produce sufficient amounts to offset losses in lumber, one of the factors in the company's decision not to extend a line to Shallotte. Between this effect and that of another movement, seeds were being sown for a major change in the road's fortunes.

Another anecdote of the time relates how a northbound train was stalled about thirteen miles away from Wilmington between Brunswick and Winnabow. As the *Wilmington Morning Star* of June 27, 1920, tells it:

> *Losing all of its strength when it was almost at its destination, the locomotive that has been pulling the passenger train on the Wilmington, Brunswick and Southern Railroad between this city and Southport for many moons stopped in the piney woods yesterday morning, causing the train to be delayed three hours in arriving at the union station. When at a point between Brunswick and Winnabow stations, Engineer Grantham, blowing his whistle in his usual attractive manner, pulled on the cord a little too hard and broke the whistle valve. In a few moments every ounce of steam in the boiler had escaped and, having no power, the engine slowed up and finally stopped. Passengers, hearing the noise of the escaping steam, craned their necks out of the windows to ascertain what had happened and were chagrined when they learned that no amount of fire in the locomotive could generate power enough to move the iron monsterette. After conferring over the matter, the train crew decided the only thing to be done was to send back to Southport for the other locomotive belonging to this railroad so one man trudged to Winnabow and telephoned the agent at the far end of the line for help.*

The tone of the news account seems to treat the incident as a comic occurrence, maybe even in the range of what one might expect from the WB&S. In another incident, perhaps a foretaste of what lay ahead, the railroad's aging trestle across Jackey's Creek, a hastily built relic from twenty years earlier, burned and had to be replaced. Otherwise, little of what the railroad did was ever reported in the mainstream press, and its operations settled in as part of the routine activity in the area. In the meantime, railroad employees did what they could to keep the old engine running as best as they could.

Seasonal shipments of shrimp, oysters and other fish also added to the volume of activity to sustain the WB&S. Local canning plants and icehouses were built near the shoreline processing plants. The *Greensboro Daily News* reported a notable record of thirty-one well-iced carloads of shrimp sent to

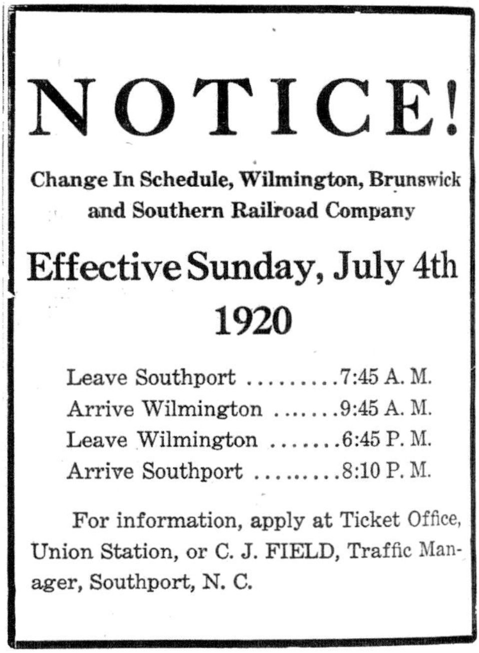

NOTICE!

Change In Schedule, Wilmington, Brunswick and Southern Railroad Company

Effective Sunday, July 4th 1920

Leave Southport ....7:45 A. M.
Arrive Wilmington ....9:45 A. M.
Leave Wilmington ....6:45 P. M.
Arrive Southport ....8:10 P. M.

For information, apply at Ticket Office, Union Station, or C. J. FIELD, Traffic Manager, Southport, N. C.

Only a single-track line, the WB&S most often ran a daily round trip to Wilmington, with an occasional accommodation train based on need. The standard schedule was subject to deviations due to the vagaries of operations and seasonal demand. Wilmington Morning Star, *July 1, 1920.*

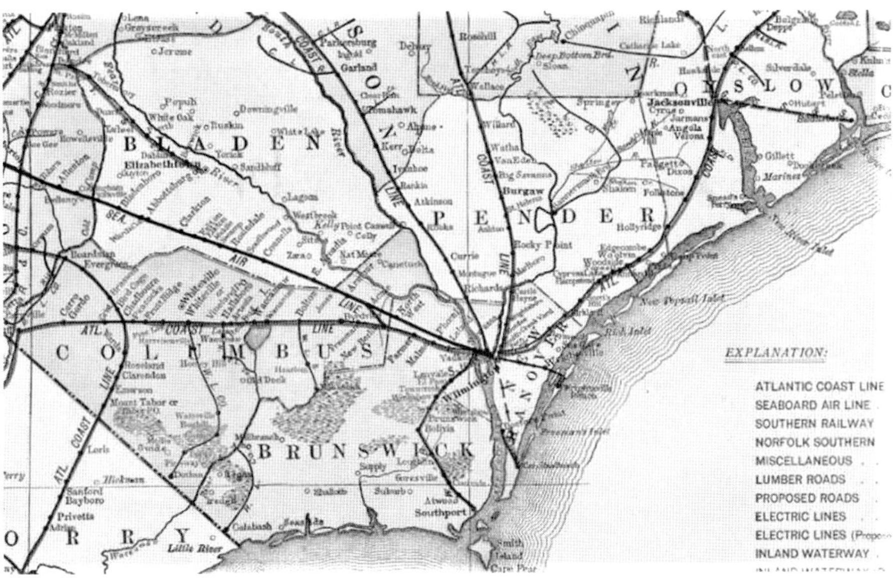

Rail routes out of Wilmington. WB&S stops or stations include Navassa, Lanvale, El Paso, Town Creek, Winnabow, Brunswick, Bolivia, Loughlin, Goresville, Coolvale, Atwood and Southport. *North Carolina Corporation Commission, "Railroad Map of North Carolina," Rand McNally and Company, detail, 1917. Courtesy of the North Carolina Department of Natural and Cultural Resources.*

Daniel L. Russell Jr. (1845–1908), the only Republican governor elected between Reconstruction years and 1972. He had a long political career—elected to the state legislature at age nineteen, serving as Superior Court judge at age twenty-three and two terms in Congress. His landholdings included Winnabow Plantation near Town Creek, established by his father in the 1840s with about twenty-five thousand acres of forest and agriculture. *State Archives of North Carolina.*

northern markets in 1922. These required special scheduling at the Navassa interchange to enable timely transfer and shipment—ideally, within twenty-four hours—to New York.

The operations of the WB&S had at least a nominal schedule, but deviations were frequent enough to earn its nickname of "Willing But Slow" or even "Wobbles, Bumps and Shakes" for the character of its insufficiently ballasted track. In the words of authors B.A. Botkin and Alvin F. Harlow in *A Treasury of Railroad Folklore*, short lines like the WB&S were "the negation of regimented uniformity, [surviving] as a triumph of individualism and even eccentricity, innocent of the trammeling devices of signaling, dispatching and traffic control of any save the most primitive sort."

So here we have a second factor in the railroad's demise: essential revenue traffic (freight) could not rise to the level needed to allow the railroad to thrive, despite the early significant growth of enterprises along its line. Marketable timber was becoming depleted, northbound products (fishmeal, shellfish, crops and the like) were subject to seasonal fluctuations and the market for southbound products was too small to generate a need for carload lots. The premise of a major coaling stop for transatlantic traffic, long held as a central justification for a rail line, never garnered enough consistent support from the powers that would have allowed it to materialize. Moreover, continued improvements at Wilmington's port diminished demand for competing facilities at Southport, contributing to the railroad's existence as essentially a shuttle.

The halcyon years were coming to a close.

Chapter 9

EMERGENCE OF COMPETING MODES

Southport had well-established river service and a railroad was now finally operating, but not much attention had been paid to the existence or condition of roads and highways in the county. Roads, such as they were, tended to serve immediate local needs, without much thought as to how they might be integrated into a transportation network. Moreover, upkeep and maintenance in the early years were expected to be voluntarily undertaken by local landowners (rather haphazardly) at the direction of township leaders. It was almost as if the prevailing philosophy was that simply having a road to one's property was like an extended driveway, and the property owner should be expected to maintain it accordingly.

The result was the gradual development of minimally cleared roads wide enough to accommodate only a single wagon or pair of horses, roughly graded (if at all) to the native grade. Moreover, road surveying was almost entirely unknown; routes tended to meander wherever the path was easiest. Early maps clearly show routes that, by today's expectations, make little sense for timely travel—although perhaps that wasn't the point at the time. For anyone wanting to get to a shipping point, living beyond eight miles from accessible transportation would be impractical, given the time needed to get there and back in the same day.

Later on, with some reluctance, road upkeep devolved on the counties. Without any form of consistency or coordination among counties, however, little was done because little could be done. For the most part, roads were still seen as bare-minimum connections to farms or settlements rather

North Carolina was at no greater disadvantage than the rest of the country. In 1919, the U.S. Army organized a Motor Transport Corps, with the mission to drive from Washington, D.C., to San Francisco. Under the command of Lieutenant Colonel Dwight Eisenhower, the unit took two months to get there (average speed of less than six miles per hour), losing vehicles and men along the way—a vivid demonstration about the poor quality of roads and highways at the time. By contrast, a train could make the trip in about four days (an average speed of about thirty-four miles per hour).

than extended routes serving convenient or commercial purposes to access major towns or shipping centers.

In Brunswick County, a few roads had been laid out in the colonial era, such as the Wilmington–Georgetown Road (roughly present-day U.S. Highway 17) and the Wilmington–Fayetteville Road (some of its route remains in use in Leland). Other random roads branched off these or paralleled the Cape Fear River along its west bank to serve a couple dozen riverside plantations. Very rarely were any of these conceived as straight lines. At the time, a trip from Smithville (Southport) to Wilmington might well take six or more hours—essentially a day-long ordeal.

Once these roads approached the last leg to Wilmington at the Brunswick River, a ferry carried traffic across to Eagle Island to the head of a graded causeway leading to the city. At its east end, another ferry took traffic across the Cape Fear River to the foot of Market Street. Altogether, this was a time-consuming process that strengthened the case for the relative convenience of a railroad link. It wouldn't be until 1890 that a decent bridge would at least span the Brunswick River to the head of the causeway.

The WB&S barely got a good start to its operations when it encountered the initiative that would have far-reaching effects—the Good Roads Movement. This was a national effort (with North Carolina forming its association in 1902), but it accelerated with passage of the Federal Road Aid Act of 1916 and the designation of roads as postal routes. North Carolina transportation activists sought to expand and improve the state's roads, aiming to connect every county seat in a network of serviceable highways. In 1915, the State Highway Commission was formed to coordinate roads and highways.

In 1918, arising from a convention of the Good Roads Association at Wrightsville Beach, the president of the association, W.A. McGirt, wrote to

Governor Thomas W. Bickett, as recorded in "The Good Roads Movement," found at www.learnnc.org:

> *North Carolina, if she would keep step with other progressive states, must wake up to the vital necessity of creating a better state-wide system of public highways,* [and] *I am appealing to you to give the movement referred to in the resolution enclosed, your undivided support and hearty co-operation.*
>
> *There is an urgent need of a State system of roads, so that the people of each county can gain easy access to these National highways, to adjoining counties and markets, and to other sections of the State and Nation.*

In 1921, the North Carolina General Assembly passed a bill to enable the state's involvement in the initiative and authorized a $40 million highway bond. Statewide coordination would have to wait until 1931, when counties would cede highway development to the state.

The movement, all in all, had worthy objectives. The automobile and its heavy-duty cousin, the truck, were becoming commonplace. Even though cities often had some paved streets on which to run vehicles, there were few good roads once one left the city limits. Joseph Hyde Pratt's article "Good Roads Movement in the South," in the *Annals of the American Academy of Political and Social Science* (January 1910), provides a glimpse of the situation in North Carolina. With nearly 50,000 miles of public roads, the state had only 475 miles of them paved, often of doubtful and undependable serviceability. Without proper construction and maintenance of roads, let alone consistent standards from county to county, road trips of any distance were arduous and fraught with perils of all types. A partial list might include potholes, washouts, mud sloughs, uneven grading, absence of signs or designations, hazards to tires and mechanical problems and uncertain fueling points. The best alternative to motoring any distance was the train, although tracks could not possibly connect all points.

Brunswick County roads, such as they were, were few and far between. The county had an area of 1,050 square miles, with about 850 deemed as "land." With much of the population concentrated in a few towns, roads tended to connect just those few points, with very large spaces between them. By 1915, the county had about 750 miles of "roads," only 48 of which could be termed as "improved," such improvements simply being a compacted overlay of shells and clay instead of the usual graded sand. Such a topping counted as a hardening, although that would be a stretched definition to justify under all conditions. Recollections from lifelong residents in Southport mention being bogged down in the fearsome "yellow clay" when it rained, and ruts could easily be up to eight inches deep.

The time it took to get from Southport to Wilmington was markedly improved once the WB&S was up and running. Even with its hastily built roadbed, the railroad offered all-weather travel, avoided perils of surface roads and could make the trip in a fraction of the time. For passengers, this meant that day trips to either city were possible, instead of having to take an entire day simply to arrive. For freight, this meant reliable transport for bulk shipments of fish and fish products, lumber and forest products, crops and produce and more. The limitation was that railroads had to operate on a schedule, and trains only ran a couple of trips a day. Within ten years, however, improved hard-surface roads would be demonstrating distinct advantages for motor traffic over the railroad experience.

A map from 1910 shows such roads branching out from Navassa and the tiny place of Leland. Roads often were named for a town where they were more or less aimed. Two in particular had existed since colonial times: Wilmington-Fayetteville Road (largely seen today as Old Fayetteville Road) and Wilmington-Georgetown Road (pretty much the route of today's U.S. Highway 17, although containing many twists and turns). Another map at the time included a very primitive River Road (more or less still existing as North Carolina Highway 133 with some deviations, notably a detour around today's Sunny Point Military Ocean Terminal). And then there were Old Brunswick and Southport Roads (branching off Wilmington–Georgetown Road to join River Road near the Old Town settlement), paths very close to defining the boundaries of the Brunswick Forest development today. Owing to creeks, swamps and numerous backwaters and ponds, many of these early roads wound laboriously through the county wherever reasonably solid footing could be found.

The Good Roads Movement continued to make progress, and in 1922, the *State Highway System of North Carolina* was published by the Virginia Engraving Company of Richmond. It showed Brunswick County with its Highway 201, overlaying straight-as-an-arrow Town Line Road inland from Southport before bending to the north at Supply at the old Wilmington-Georgetown Road. At the time, the "improved" Southport-Supply Road was only about eight feet wide, generating innumerable arguments when opposing vehicles met and one needed to yield to let the other pass on. A surface of packed clay and shells was only marginally better than native soil, but at least it provided a definite path between the two towns.

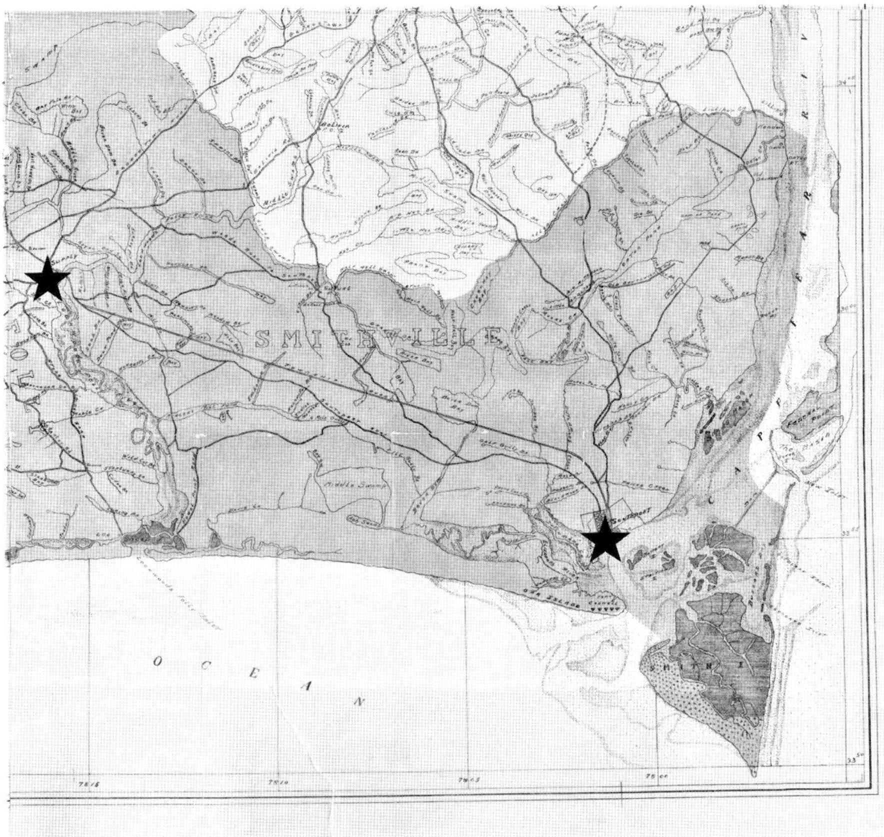

This map of Brunswick County (*Southport at lower center*) shows only one road of recent construction, laid on a straight line from Southport (*lower star*) to Supply (*upper star*), now designated NC Highway 211. Other roads show the earlier practice of building meandering roads more for convenience than durability to connect small settlements and plantations. *Charles Henry Smith, "Map of Brunswick County," detail, 1910. State Archives of North Carolina.*

Having a surface highway allowed much easier farm-to-market connections, opened up new areas for development and improved business travel (Southport was still the county seat) and general transportation. Moreover, the advent of good roads allowed unscheduled travel anytime, as opposed to being dependent on the railroad's sometimes unpredictable timetable and limited station stops.

Although it had been advocated since 1910, it wasn't until 1920 that the causeway across Eagles Island into Wilmington was satisfactorily paved to make that passage much easier. The erection of bridges across both branches of the Cape Fear River was finally accomplished in 1929 to

What passed for a better road in Brunswick County in the late 1910s. This is the Southport-Supply Road (now designated as NC 211), widened from an earlier time but nowhere near durable. Fortunately, cars of the time usually rode high enough to compensate for the depth of ruts in the soft surface. State Port Pilot, *"The Way It Was" series.*

complete a continuous motor route from Southport to Wilmington. This also represented a permanent escape from the schedule of the WB&S for shippers and travelers.

The WB&S saw its fortunes start to decline as improved roads supplanted its position as the way to get from Wilmington to Southport. For one thing, its line was simply not long enough to offer an advantage in travel time to Wilmington. And with only one train a day, freight and passenger service could not compete with the anytime possibilities of improved roads. Additional, more convenient options were now available. There were still calls for carload lots of freight (or, more frequently, less-than-carload lots) to be transported from one terminus to the other, but much of the in-between occasional and seasonal loads were finding alternative means to move.

The effects of the Good Roads Movement were felt across the state. Reports from the North Carolina Corporation Commission noted fifty-seven railroads operating within the state in 1921; just a couple of years later in 1923, that number had dropped to forty-six. More signs of the times were noted as significant decreases in passenger traffic drew mention in its 1927–28 biennial report, and there was mention of many more petitions

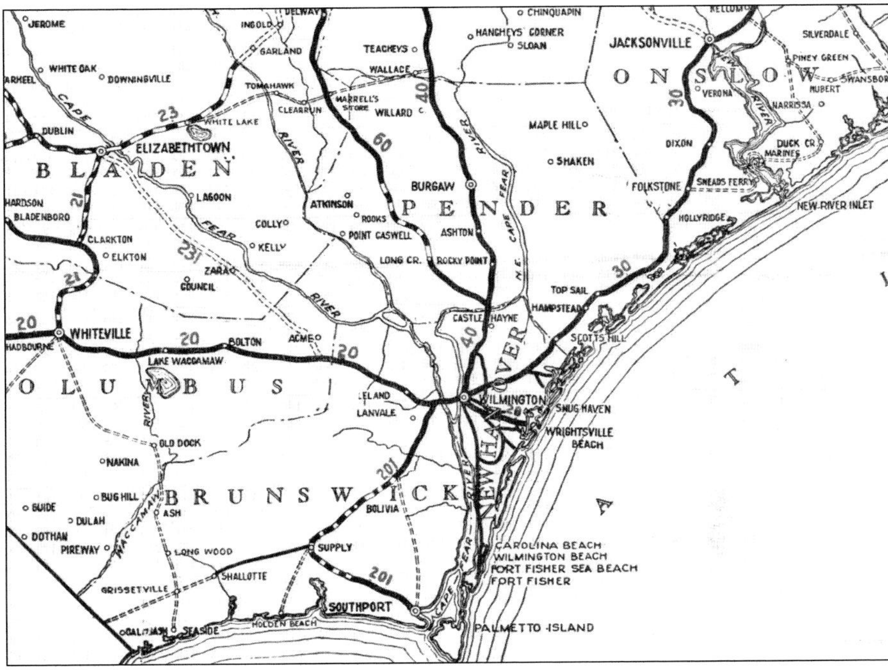

In Brunswick County in 1926, Highway 201 ran from Southport to Wilmington (now defined by U.S. Highway 17 and NC Highway 211). The map legend indicates that only the northern and southern segments were hard surfaced; in between were miles of packed clay and shell material. What is now NC Highway 87 is drawn as little more than a dirt road; the WB&S route lies between the two highways. *North Carolina State Highway Commission, "State Highway System of North Carolina," detail, Bynum Printing Company, 1926. State Archives of North Carolina.*

for closures of stations and agencies in 1929. Passenger revenues naturally followed suit; there was a 25 percent decrease between 1930 ($10.4 million) and 1931 ($7.9 million).

So a third factor in the demise of the WB&S was the development of improved roadways that diminished the need for a fixed point-to-point railway with limited access. As roads were developed, they largely surpassed the advantages of rail. It was no longer necessary to depend on once-a-day service to get goods to market, and they could be transported from anywhere along the roadways, at any time. This was hardly a unique situation. Throughout the country, roads were rapidly being improved to handle the burgeoning supply of automobiles. Many short lines throughout the nation, once established to provide reliable and accessible transportation to narrow geographic areas, found themselves in similar circumstances when improved and durable roads and vehicles eliminated their advantages.

Chapter 10

ADJUSTMENTS IN THE 1920s

The decade of the 1920s started on a reasonably bright note. As noted at its annual meeting, the WB&S sold forty thousand passenger fares in 1919, likely the high-water mark for that service. The company had published fares of $1.40 for the thirty-mile trip, and with twelve potential stopping points between Wilmington and Southport, access was convenient all along the route. M.J. Corbett was elected president of the company, probably not anticipating the sad turn of events in the coming years.

As noted in the *Wilmington Morning Star* of January 30, 1921, fourteen sawmills along the route shipped all of their product by rail, generating an average of about 150 carloads of lumber per month, along with fishmeal and seafood shipments from Southport. After ten years of use, however, the WB&S was starting to see its operations deteriorate. Like so many other railroads, whether short lines or major carriers, maintenance issues tended to be deferred in favor of day-to-day needs. In addition, there may have been some residual effects from financial shenanigans related to the Town Creek Lumber Company a few years before.

In 1921, the officers of the WB&S petitioned the Interstate Commerce Commission for a loan of $200,000 (local banks by this time were refusing credit). They were able to secure a five-year note for $90,000, which they intended to invest in repairs and upgrades. Trestles across creeks, among the earliest structures from before the turn of the century, were weakening, and the company's remaining engine was showing its age. Fort Caswell, where soldiers provided reliable passenger demand, had pretty well been shut down and decommissioned.

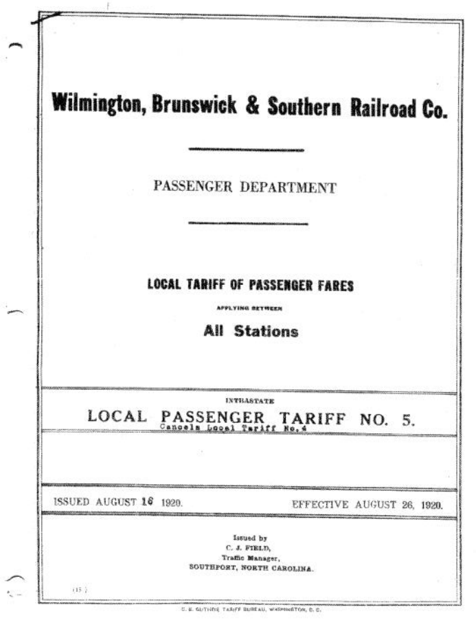

Wilmington, Brunswick & Southern Railroad Co.

PASSENGER DEPARTMENT

LOCAL TARIFF OF PASSENGER FARES

APPLYING BETWEEN

All Stations

INTRASTATE

LOCAL PASSENGER TARIFF NO. 5.

Cancels Local Tariff No. 4

ISSUED AUGUST 16 1920. EFFECTIVE AUGUST 26, 1920.

Issued by
C. J. FIELD,
Traffic Manager,
SOUTHPORT, NORTH CAROLINA.

C. E. GUTHRIE TARIFF BUREAU, WASHINGTON, D. C.

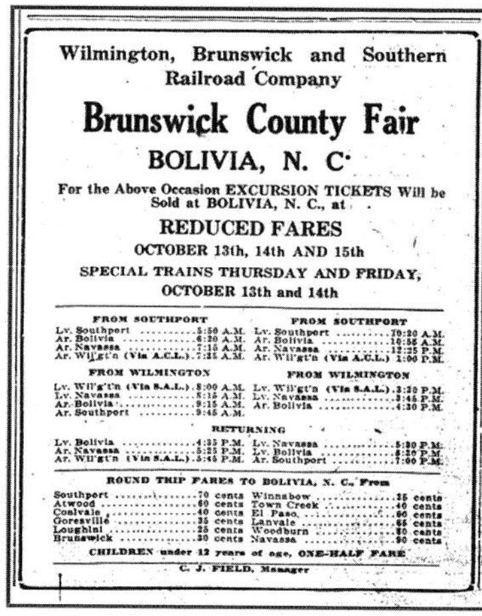

Wilmington, Brunswick and Southern Railroad Company

Brunswick County Fair

BOLIVIA, N. C.

For the Above Occasion EXCURSION TICKETS Will be Sold at BOLIVIA, N. C., at

REDUCED FARES

OCTOBER 13th, 14th AND 15th

SPECIAL TRAINS THURSDAY AND FRIDAY, OCTOBER 13th and 14th

FROM SOUTHPORT

Lv. Southport ....5:50 A.M.
Ar. Bolivia ....6:20 A.M.
Ar. Navassa ....7:15 A.M.
Ar. Wil'gt'n (Via A.C.L.) 7:25 A.M.

FROM SOUTHPORT

Lv. Southport ....10:20 A.M.
Ar. Bolivia ....10:55 A.M.
Ar. Navassa ....12:25 P.M.
Ar. Wil'gt'n (Via A.C.L.) 1:00 P.M.

FROM WILMINGTON

Lv. Wil'g't'n (Via S.A.L.) 8:00 A.M.
Lv. Navassa ....8:15 A.M.
Ar. Bolivia ....9:15 A.M.
Ar. Southport ....9:45 A.M.

FROM WILMINGTON

Lv. Wil'gt'n (Via S.A.L.) 3:30 P.M.
Lv. Navassa ....3:45 P.M.
Ar. Bolivia ....4:30 P.M.

RETURNING

Lv. Bolivia ....4:35 P.M.
Ar. Navassa ....5:25 P.M.
Ar. Wil'gt'n (Via S.A.L.) 5:45 P.M.

Lv. Navassa ....5:30 P.M.
Lv. Bolivia ....6:20 P.M.
Ar. Southport ....7:00 P.M.

ROUND TRIP FARES TO BOLIVIA, N. C., From

Southport ....70 cents
Atwood ....60 cents
Coolvale ....40 cents
Goresville ....35 cents
Loughlin ....25 cents
Brunswick ....30 cents
Winnabow ....35 cents
Town Creek ....40 cents
El Paso ....60 cents
Lanvale ....65 cents
Woodburn ....80 cents
Navassa ....90 cents

CHILDREN under 12 years of age, ONE-HALF FARE

C. J. FIELD, Manager

Left: Published schedule of WB&S passenger fares, 1920. *Author's collection.*

Right: The WB&S was still able to offer expanded passenger service in 1921, when extra trains to the Brunswick County Fair were scheduled. Before too much longer, better roads made access by car or truck much more convenient, although the fair itself lasted just one more year. Wilmington Morning Star, *October 1921.*

The year 1921 also saw two incidents that dented the company's fragile finances. In May, a Southport-bound mixed consist train derailed near Coolvale, today a pocket neighborhood between State Highway 87 and the headwaters of Dutchman Creek north of Southport. There were no significant injuries among the passengers on the train, but a tank car tipped and spilled nearly ten thousand gallons of oil, and the accident tore up about two hundred yards of track, requiring immediate cleanup and repair work. Passengers were put aboard a freight car for the remainder of the trip into Southport. In addition, Wilmington Iron Works sued the WB&S in December for $1,300 to cover repair work on its engines.

The WB&S also began losing some of its founders and perhaps a bit of the spirit of the company's initial enthusiasm. In 1922, A.J. McKinnon, a significant figure in agriculture and commodities around Laurinburg, died. A year later saw the passing of Z.W. Whitehead, who was a tireless proponent of the WB&S and served as its president for many years. George Bellamy died in 1924 after a fall off the porch of the Orton Hotel in Wilmington.

Transient attention was paid to a rumor in 1923 that Henry Ford had an interest in developing a rail route from the Pocahontas coal fields in Virginia and West Virginia. The path would travel south through Mount

Airy, Winston-Salem and thence on a direct line to Southport. Apparently, the grand vision of a Southport coaling station was not quite dead yet, sputtering along on a few residual embers. At about the same time, however, the Atlantic Coast Line was already in discussions to lease the Clinchfield & Ohio Railroad. Since this was an established coal carrier serving the same area, that lease essentially foreclosed Ford's idea.

It was also reported that only five or six cars of holly had been shipped to northern markets, although even this was an irregular occurrence. Apparently, the desirable berries did not appear every year, so there would have been some years with no such shipments. It was a far cry from the three hundred to five hundred carloads of holly shipped to northern markets several years earlier.

In 1924, the company bought a so-called oil burner locomotive by Baldwin for $12,800 from Georgia Car & Locomotive Company, a dealer and parts supplier in Atlanta, Georgia. It may very well have been that the old wood-burning locomotive (#100) had finally given up, and they used a portion of their 1921 loan to upgrade their motive power. As an additional benefit, this engine did not produce hot embers and reduced the perennial aggravation of fires along the grassy right-of-way. They also built a ten-thousand-gallon fuel tank to eliminate the need for pumping from tank cars stored on side tracks. This ten-wheeler was numbered #101 and put to work in freight service, although less often as the years went on and eventually relegated to idle track at the end of the line. Weighing in at about fifty tons, it also likely put a strain on the lightweight tracks and bed, which had not been improved from its packed sand-and-clay construction.

Later that year, the WB&S initiated motorcar service on its line with a Brill GM68 combine, a self-powered light transit unit resembling a trolley car. Designated as #11, this would carry passengers and mail to Navassa, where they would transfer to a bus for the last leg into Wilmington, via the Eagle Island causeway and ferry. The advantage was that motorcar service did not entail firing an engine and coupling cars, and it could be accomplished outside the freight schedule, allowing travelers more time in Wilmington. In addition, only a driver/conductor was needed to operate the motorcar, instead of a two-man crew for the locomotive-headed trains. At the outset, three round trips daily were anticipated. Track inspection and routine maintenance were handled out of the station. For this purpose, an old automobile had been stripped down and fitted with rail-compatible wheels to ride out along the track, a common method of repurposing among railroads.

In new service is the very shiny WB&S #101, purchased in 1924. This was a five-year-old Baldwin ten-wheeler sold by the Georgia Car & Locomotive Company in Atlanta, Georgia, where the picture was taken. *From the collection of Donald R. Hensley Jr., www.taplines.net.*

From a grainy photograph, a drawing of WB&S #11, a Brill GM68 motorcar (or railcar). Likely painted dark green, this steel-body unit could also carry small cargo and the mail, seated about twenty passengers and had an onboard toilet compartment. In the absence of scheduled freight, this would be the only unit on the tracks for a daily run to Wilmington. *Drawn by author from source image.*

> To alleviate rolling stock supply and congestion issues surrounding mobilization for World War I, the government formed the United States Railroad Administration (USRA) in 1917. While many enduring benefits were instituted, the USRA came in for its share of criticism. Among other practices, it prioritized war-related freight, raised passenger fares, raised workforce wages, deferred infrastructure improvements and relegated company profits to secondary importance. The USRA expired in 1920, although railroads spent several years recovering from its management.

Freight service continued with the railroad's single locomotive, and shipments of fish, seafood and fish products were seasonally very demanding. In 1925, about 200,000 gallons of fish oil went out from the processing plants nearby, along with near-daily shipments of raw iced shrimp or canned shrimp and oysters. These would have been dropped off in Navassa to be transported farther by the Atlantic Coast Line or Seaboard Air Line.

The WB&S operated freight and small-scale passenger runs that were subject to variation at scheduled and flag stops along its route. Brunswick County was still in slow motion, as gathered from an oral history project of the University of North Carolina–Wilmington in 1995. Robert Shannon, one of the sons of station manager Hubert Shannon, recalled that, even with the railroad's erratic travel times, it was sardonically characterized as "the fastest thing in the county." In 1926, it did have a timetable showing a single northbound and southbound train each day, but its operations were somewhat on the casual side, and deviations from its published schedule were common. In a taped interview with lifelong resident Lilly Morrill with Don and Betty Johnson (1991), one anecdote relates how the engineer on the southbound train forgot to pick up a passenger at Bolivia, so he decided to back up the train from Southport to get her.

Small changes and practices like these were symptoms of the larger forces at work as North Carolina upgraded its roads and improved port facilities at Wilmington. One might wonder whether the WB&S management ever approached the Atlantic Coast Line or Seaboard Air Line Railroads to get some relief from its growing woes. This could have been in the form of a capital infusion for a stake in the company, selling its line of track and paying only trackage fees or perhaps even an outright sale.

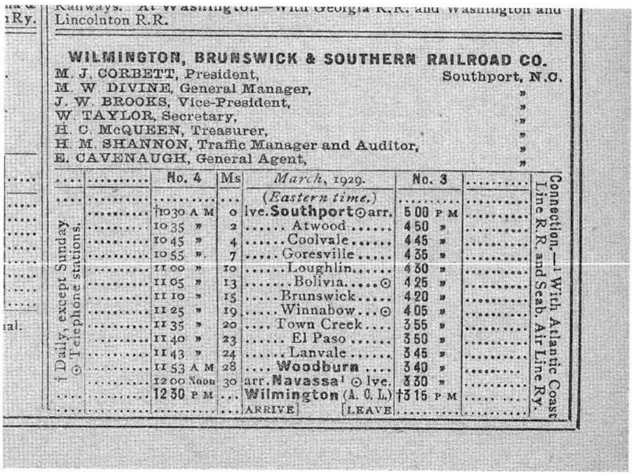

WILMINGTON, BRUNSWICK & SOUTHERN RAILROAD CO.

M. J. CORBETT, President, Southport, N.C.
M. W. DIVINE, General Manager, "
J. W. BROOKS, Vice-President, "
W. TAYLOR, Secretary, "
H. C. McQUEEN, Treasurer, "
H. M. SHANNON, Traffic Manager and Auditor, "
E. CAVENAUGH, General Agent, "

No. 4	Ms	March, 1929. (Eastern time.)	No. 3
†10 30 A M	0	lve. **Southport** ⊙ arr.	5 00 P M
10 35 "	2	Atwood	4 50 "
10 45 "	4	Coolvale	4 45 "
10 55 "	7	Goresville	4 35 "
11 00 "	10	Loughlin	4 30 "
11 05 "	13	Bolivia ⊙	4 25 "
11 10 "	15	Brunswick	4 20 "
11 25 "	19	Winnabow ⊙	4 05 "
11 35 "	20	Town Creek	3 55 "
11 40 "	23	El Paso	3 50 "
11 43 "	24	Lanvale	3 45 "
11 53 A M	28	**Woodburn**	3 40 "
12 00 Noon	30	arr. **Navassa**[1] ⊙ lve.	3 30 "
12 30 P M		**Wilmington** (A. C. L.)	†3 15 P M
		ARRIVE] [LEAVE	

† Daily, except Sunday. ⊙ Telephone stations.

Connection.—[1] With Atlantic Coast Line R.R. and Seab. Air Line Ry.

In 1929, the WB&S still listed a schedule for passenger service, but deviations from posted times would have been common. At least there were still the trappings of an organization, with several longtime officers of the company listed. Official Guide of the Railways, *National Railway Publication Company, 1929. Courtesy of Wilmington Railroad Museum.*

Swimming near the WB&S coal dock, 1920s. Currents, debris, tides and maybe even the occasional shark made this a dicey pastime, but the river was the place to go for a refreshing dip in warm weather. Some years later, a floating platform was anchored off the skinny strip of riverbank sand that served as a beach. State Port Pilot, *"The Way It Was" series.*

Whatever the situation, there don't seem to be any indications of interest from either of the big companies. Like so many other large rail operators, they had spent the early 1920s recovering from the problematic management of the railroads by the federal government in World War I and the few years afterward (1917–20). It would be unlikely that they would have much interest in gaining control of or acquiring a thirty-mile local spur line with (a) shrinking business operating on a (b) deteriorating roadbed with (c) aging equipment.

Throughout the decade, it seems the WB&S was left on its own, unable to recapitalize or effectively gain new business and cobbling together what business it could find to keep it afloat. It was still making claims of accomplishing its trips in ninety minutes. By now, however, that exceeded more convenient highway alternatives by a considerable amount.

In 1926, the WB&S no longer was listed in the Wilmington City Directory (nor was its host, M.W. Divine Co., at the 23 Market Street location). It is presumed that the railroad withdrew its management and agency functions to Southport, perhaps as an economizing measure, in another small instance of shrinking operations. In Wilmington, the railroad was likely represented by a part-time agent in borrowed office space, if there was any agent at all.

Things weren't looking so good.

Chapter 11

THE END

At the outset, the WB&S had been reduced to serving narrow geographic interests along a short route. It then fell to the successful introduction of improved roads and highways, which offered more effective and efficient modes of transport for products and passengers. Chronically undercapitalized and over-leveraged, its destiny was essentially sealed when it could not gain significant financial support—and then the country entered the Great Depression, spreading its effects far and wide, including all aspects of the railroad industry.

To scale back on operational costs, the company in 1931 bought a Plymouth Model WL diesel locomotive and labeled it #600. Built in 1928, it had been rented by three industrial users in as many years. Happily, it was much lighter than locomotive #101, providing some relief to the company's deteriorating railbed and rails. It wasn't speedy, although that probably suited the WB&S just fine. Its 165-horsepower engine transmitted power through a mechanical transmission to a clanking chain drive for the wheels. It was also far better suited to the irregular and occasional trips that constituted the company's "schedule" in these last years.

In 1932, the railroad claimed 24 employees, but it is doubtful that any of these were full-timers. In its report to the North Carolina Corporation Commission, the company's operating revenue of $918 per mile was insufficient to offset expenses of $929 per mile. At this point, it still registered 1,954 passenger trips on its aging motorcar (down from 20,000 in 1919), but that averaged a mere 6 passengers a day to generate 28

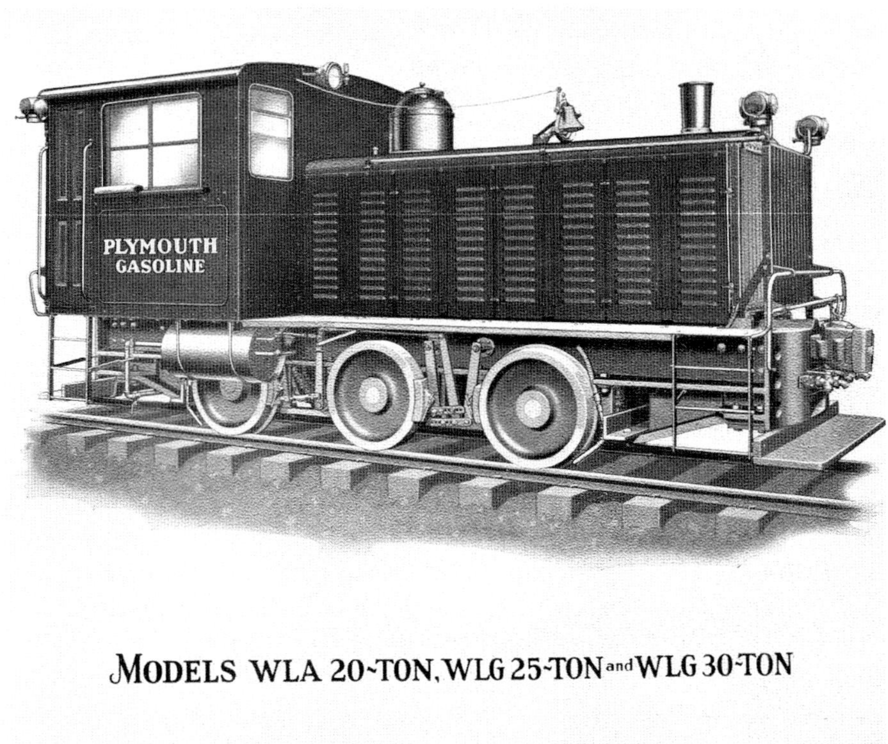

Above: In its last years, the WB&S operated a Plymouth industrial locomotive, here shown in a catalogue image. It was slow and clunky but was much lighter than the company's ten-wheeler and far easier on the fragile railway. *American Industrial Mining Company Museum, AIM Co. Museum Library.*

Opposite: Annual report from WB&S to North Carolina Corporation Commission, 1932. *Author's collection.*

percent of the company's already insufficient revenues. Indeed, for most people, the highways that had been built years earlier were far superior to train service and were much more convenient and reliable than the railroad's once-a-day schedule.

The company couldn't set aside sufficient funds to reinvest in equipment and infrastructure, and revenue from freight service never achieved sufficient volume to sustain the venture. Any hope for additional capital pretty much dried up with the Great Depression. Finally, it is very likely that neither of the nearby companies with service to Wilmington (Atlantic Coast Line and Seaboard Air Line) would have been interested in bailing out and reinvesting in the WB&S, given their own financial challenges.

REPORT

OF THE

Wilmington, Brunswick & Southern R.R. COMPANY

TO THE

NORTH CAROLINA CORPORATION COMMISSION

FOR THE YEAR ENDING DECEMBER 31, 1931

1. Name of Company Wilmington, Brunswick & Southern Railroad Company
2. Date of Organization January 22, 1907
3. Under Laws of What State North Carolina

Give reference to each Statute General Laws

AUG 13 1932
CORPORATION COMMISSION

OFFICERS

TITLE	NAME	LOCATION OF OFFICE
President	M.J. Corbett	Wilmington N.C
General Manager ~~or Superintendent~~	M. W Divine	" "
Secretary ~~and Treasurer~~	Walker Taylor	" "
Treasurer	John D. Corbett	" "
Traffic Manager	H M Shannon	Southport N.C.

DIRECTORS AND ADDRESSES

M J Corbett, Wilmington N.C. S. J Springer, Wilmington N.C.
M W Divine " " Walker Taylor "
H.C. McQueen " "
J. W. Brooks " "

PROPERTY OPERATED

FROM	TO	MILES N.C.	MILES TOTAL
Navassa N.C	Southport, N.C.	30.2	30.2

Capital Stock	$165,000.00
Capital Stock, per mile	5,463.59
Funded Debt	183,750.00
Funded Debt, per mile	6,084.44
Cost of Road	464,040.31
Cost of Road, per mile	15,365.57
Cost of Equipment	27,498.61
Cost of Equipment, per mile	910.55
Cost of Road and Equipment, per mile	16,276.12
Operating Revenue	27,722.08
Operating Expenses (Interest on bonds not included)	28,044.30
Net Operating Revenue	322.22
Operating Revenue, per mile	917.95
Operating Expenses, per mile	928.62
Total Freight Revenue	18,016.59
Total Passenger Train Service Revenue	7,193.57
Freight Revenue, per mile	596.68
Total Number Passengers Carried Earning Revenue	1,954
Passenger Service Train Revenue, per mile	238.20
Revenue from Other Sources	2,511.92
Average Receipts per Passenger, per mile	.0306
Taxes Paid, N. C.	[illegible]

In its 1932 report of the WB&S to the North Carolina Corporation Commission, the company listed just six directors, led by M.J. Corbett as president. Others included M.W. Divine (general manager), Walker Taylor (secretary), John D. Corbett (treasurer), H.C. McQueen, J.W. Brooks and S.J. Springer. Of these, Corbett, Divine and McQueen had been part of the original group of principals. They would likely have been glumly considering

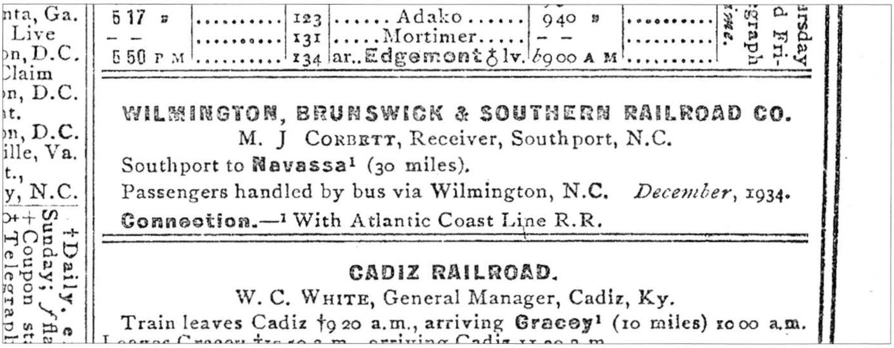

5 17 »	....	123	...... Adako	9 40 »	....
– –	....	131	..... Mortimer.....	– –	....
5 50 P M	....	134	ar.. Edgemont ♂ lv.	b9 00 A M	....

WILMINGTON, BRUNSWICK & SOUTHERN RAILROAD CO.
M. J CORBETT, Receiver, Southport, N.C.
Southport to **Navassa**[1] (30 miles).
Passengers handled by bus via Wilmington, N.C. *December*, 1934.
Connection.—[1] With Atlantic Coast Line R.R.

CADIZ RAILROAD.
W. C. WHITE, General Manager, Cadiz, Ky.
Train leaves Cadiz †9 20 a.m., arriving **Gracey**[1] (10 miles) 10 00 a.m.

In its twilight years, the WB&S passenger schedule was virtually nonexistent, with rides being furnished by bus instead of over the rails. For the WB&S (now in receivership), this was just a sign of winding down as roads were improved and private automobiles allowed freer travel. Official Guide of the Railways, *National Railway Publication Company, 1934. Courtesy of Wilmington Railroad Museum.*

the railroad's business, which generated $27,722 in revenue against $28,044 in expenses—a small but portentous loss of $322. Nineteen employees were now reported, likely using a generous definition of what constituted employment.

Passenger traffic slowed to nearly nothing, and freight service was just an occasional exercise, a few cars every so often. Fish processing was still going on, but motor freight provided a much more attractive option for those companies, which themselves were hit by the Great Depression. At times, the railroad would bring in a carload of "relief flour" to distribute to those in need.

Telegraph service was still managed at the Southport station, and transcription of incoming messages and sending were handled by station personnel. Delivery of messages relied on the availability of the local manager's sons. William Shannon related in a 2002 article that the task of where to deliver them was based on their knowledge of the town, since Southport apparently had not yet established a uniform system of street addresses within its modest confines.

In 1933, the WB&S again dipped into the red according to its report to the North Carolina Corporation Commission. Revenues of $14,583 were nowhere near enough to meet expenses of $30,077—a loss of $15,494. At this point, rail passenger service was discontinued. In its stead, the company obtained the franchise for a combination bus service for passengers and the mail. Daily over-the-road runs provided convenience for the tiny trickle of passengers that remained, as noted by local historian Susie Carson in

Above: With suspension of daily service in the 1930s, the WB&S fulfilled its mail contract with the 1934 Chevrolet "bus" shown here, with driver Rollie Walton. A few passengers could also ride along on the much better roads that had been built. State Port Pilot, *"The Way It Was" series.*

Right: This vehicle, a 1936 modified stretch Chevrolet truck, replaced the vintage "woody" station wagon purchased a couple years before. State Port Pilot, *"The Way It Was" series.*

one of her "A Bit of History" columns (2004). The balance sheet showed liabilities exceeding assets by more than $275,000, and Wilmington Savings & Trust (trustee for the now-defaulted 1911 bond issue) appointed M.J. Corbett as receiver for the railroad, assisted by Hubert Shannon as auditor and traffic manager.

The railbed and infrastructure were failing; indeed, there were locations where it was downright hazardous. Some parts had been built in the 1890s, and decades of general neglect were evident on the deteriorating line. Lilly Morrill, in the afore-referenced taped interview, recalled her father, an engineer on the WB&S in the mid-1930s, who picked up some workers in Navassa who were bound for the Civilian Conservation Corps Camp Sapona at the edge of Southport:

> *My daddy picked up* [the CCC boys] *in Navassa.... When they got to Town Creek...he knew the trestle was not in real good shape, and so the boys had been ordered to get off the train out of the cars when they were coming across the trestle. And my daddy said, "I just decided if it was dangerous for them, it was dangerous for me." So he just put the train in low, whatever he did so it would just crawl along, and he got with the CC boys....He got off too, he went on and jumped back on* [the train] *and brought 'em on in.*

Late in 1935, the company applied for a trucking franchise to augment its rail capabilities. Implicit is that road transportation was proving to be a better option than railroad service for all the less-than-carload quantities to be shipped. It clearly would be much less expensive to operate a couple of express trucks on existing improved roadways than to invest in failing roadbeds and equipment (even if capital could be raised in the middle of a depression). In 1936, the WB&S began truck service with daily hauling of small freight and express both ways between Wilmington and Southport. (Dan Shannon, another son of WB&S auditor Hubert Shannon, was employed as one of the truck drivers.) The company's locomotive #101 was idled out of service on a siding; with increasingly rare use and hazardous track, it made little sense to ever fire it up again.

By the end of 1937, the WB&S was nominally operating only one locomotive, its #600 Plymouth diesel, and had an inactive and decrepit "fleet" of two passenger cars and two freight cars. Now there were only nineteen part-time employees, the majority likely in the trucking arm of operations, since rail service was nonexistent. Interest on its 1911 bond issue of $300,000 was in default, and the

> Hubert Shannon would himself be a petitioner against the company, claiming back pay for several years owed to him by the company. Times were hard as the railroad wound down. With a family to provide for, he did part-time bookkeeping for a local merchant and was paid in groceries so his family could be fed. For a few years, his sons were employed as messenger boys for ten dollars a month. He had worked for the Atlantic Coast Line and Charlotte Harbor & Northern (Florida) Railroads and joined the WB&S in 1923.

In 1938, old WB&S #101 deteriorates at its final resting place on a siding in Southport, next to its empty water and fuel tanks. Likely parked there many years earlier, it was eventually hauled away to be scrapped and recycled to support the war effort in the 1940s. *Author's collection.*

1921 note of $90,000 was still outstanding, despite having been extended from 1926 to 1931. The company had already been in receivership for some years, its balance sheet had not improved and it had been showing operating deficits for over ten years. There were still shareholders, but no dividends had been paid for many years, if ever. In 1938, all scheduled freight service was discontinued, and the railway continued to deteriorate.

Corporate officers at this time included M.J. Corbett as president (and also receiver), J.W. Brooks as vice president, M.W. Divine as general manager, Walker Taylor as secretary, H.C. McQueen as treasurer, Hubert Shannon as auditor and Robert W. Davis as general counsel. Directors still included Corbett, Taylor, McQueen, Divine and Brooks, along with S.J. Springer. Some of these were "bookending" their tenure with the railroad with its decline.

The only structure to speak of was the old station at Southport. Perhaps it was still used for ticketing and accommodating the tiny trickle of passengers on the company's "bus," but the building was being used mostly for storage.

Shown in derelict condition about 1935, the WB&S diesel locomotive #600, next to the Old Smithville Burying Ground in Southport. This was used for the increasingly rare freight trips in the final years of the company's operation. State Port Pilot, *"The Way It Was" series.*

In August 1940, a fire broke out in the rear of the station soon after some workers had left the building. As reported in the *State Port Pilot*, the blaze grew and spread to an adjacent warehouse that, among other things, held gasoline and an ammonia tank. An explosion occurred when the fire reached the tanks, causing serious injuries to two bystanders, one of whom later died of his injuries. The fire taxed the capabilities of Southport's single fire truck, which reportedly ran out of gas before it could get to the scene. Volunteer firefighters were able to salvage a portion of the building, but by that time, it was little more than a fire-damaged shell. Symbolically, the loss of the station drove home the fact that Southport's railroading days were over.

As a last effort, Hubert Shannon, H.B. Smith and state senator S.B. Frink of Southport, along with several investors from Charleston, South Carolina, incorporated the Southport Railroad and Transportation Company in 1941. Described by *The Robesonian* of January 30, 1941, the company was formed to manage the last vestiges of the railroad's trucking operation. Shannon had been with the WB&S for many years and, as auditor, would have known the most about the transportation business, but he died that year. With only $5,000 in capitalization, the new company carried on for just a few more years.

In short order, the line was finally out of operation. In 1942, WB&S-branded bus service was reintroduced, but the next year saw the sale of all the railroad's property: rails, ties, appurtenances and fixtures, roadway structures, buildings, equipment, rolling stock, right-of-way, real estate and motive power. Also sold was the franchise, which, under its name, retained bus service with two repurposed school buses. Rails, parts and ties were sold off, along with real estate, to three principal buyers for $72,500. When the rails, ties and hardware had been thoroughly removed, the company applied to the Interstate Commerce Commission for abandonment, characterizing its operation as "hopelessly insolvent," as reported in *The Robesonian* of August 2, 1943. Buyers included the Machine Tool & Equipment Co. of New York (rails, infrastructure, machinery, equipment, bus franchise—$48,500), J.D. Orrell of Wilmington and Dr. L.C. Fergus

In 1940, the warehouse behind the station caught fire and exploded the gasoline and ammonia tanks stored inside. Claiming one fatality, the fire made the station unusable, and it was demolished a short time later. The site eventually was subdivided for residential lots. State Port Pilot, *"The Way It Was" series.*

Southport's first and only fire truck for many years, purchased in 1923. This was the only motorized piece of equipment to respond to the WB&S station fire in 1940. State Port Pilot, *"The Way It Was" series.*

of Southport (real estate and other property). For a while after removal of the WB&S tracks, several short narrow-gauge tram roads remained to work adjacent forest tracts and bring out timber. The clean-up was very thorough; other than vestiges of cleared right-of-way, no evidence of the road's presence remains—no rails, no plates and joiners, no spikes, no track apparatus, no ties, no bits of metal anywhere.

During World War II, bus passenger traffic was reasonably stable and even strong enough to establish a second bus route to Whiteville, at first using repurposed school buses. In addition, the company retained its mail contract, making twice-a-day runs between Wilmington and Southport. In 1945, a vacant automobile service station was purchased to be rebuilt as a maintenance garage and passenger station once wartime constraints were

W.B.& S. BUS LINE

SOUTHPORT, N. C.

The Following Schedule Will Go Into Effect, Friday, March 1, 1946

— DAILY SCHEDULE —

LEAVE		A.M.	A.M.	P.M.	P.M.	P.M.
Southport ..	Lv.	7:00	9:00	1:30	3:45	6:00
Supply	Lv.	7:30	9:30		4:15	6:30
Bolivia	Lv.	7:45	9:45		4:30	6:45
Winnabow,	Lv.	8:00	10:00	2:00	4:45	7:00
Lanvale	Lv.	8:15	10:15	2:15	5:00	7:15
Wilmington,	Ar.	8:30	10:30	2:30	5:15	7:30

LEAVE							
Wilmington,	Lv.	7:00	9:30	1:35	4:00	6:20	10:00
Lanvale	Lv.	7:15	9:45	1:50	4:15	6:35	10:15
Winnabow,	Lv.	7:30	10:00	2:05	4:30	6:50	10:30
Bolivia	Lv.	7:45	10:15	2:20	4:45	7:05	10:45
Supply	Lv.	8:00	10:30	2:35	5:00	7:20	11:00
Southport	Ar.	8:30	11:00	3:05	5:30	7:50	11:30

— SUNDAY SCHEDULE —

LEAVE		A.M.	A.M.	P.M.	P.M.
Southport ..	Lv.	7:30	10:45	3:45	6:00
Supply	Lv.	8:00	11:15	4:15	6:30
Bolivia	Lv.	8:15	11:30	4:30	6:45
Winnabow,	Lv.	8:30	11:45	4:45	7:00
Lanvale	Lv.	8:45	12:00	5:00	7:15
Wilmington,	Ar.	9:00	12:15	5:15	7:30

LEAVE					
Wilmington,	Lv.	9:00	1:35	6:20	10:00
Lanvale	Lv.	9:15	1:50	6:35	10:15
Winnabow,	Lv.	9:30	2:05	6:50	10:30
Bolivia	Lv.	9:45	2:20	7:05	10:45
Supply	Lv.	9:55	2:35	7:20	11:00
Southport	Ar.	10:15	3:05	7:50	11:30

The WB&S managed to keep its name alive with bus service and the mail contract. In addition to trips between Southport and Wilmington, a route between Southport and Whiteville ran a bus once a day. There are no published schedules after 1948; presumably, the buses stopped running sometime that year or the next. State Port Pilot, *"The Way It Was" series.*

eased. In the next couple of years, three new buses were purchased, in a modern style similar to Greyhound or Trailways coaches. The company was running five or six daily round trips to Wilmington, with another one to Whiteville, and passenger and mail service were eventually extended to Long Beach (now Oak Island) and Holden Beach. After 1949, however, no mention can be found of the company or its schedule—the line is assumed to have folded.

Top: The WB&S bus station, which provided passenger service during World War II and into the late 1940s. The schedule had several round trips daily to Wilmington and later expanded its service to Whiteville. State Port Pilot, *"The Way It Was" series.*

Bottom: Another view of the Southport train station, this time appearing in a real estate promotion brochure, 1920. State Port Pilot, *"The Way It Was" series.*

In 1945, formal notice was at last given that the railroad route was officially abandoned. Physical traces of the roadbed would linger on for some time before surrounding developments effaced them as well. The record of its existence would be relegated to compilation maps, where old place names and former railroad rights-of-way are still marked or can be discerned from the configuration of property lines. At least as late as 1960, however, its route could still be used as a reference point, such as when a map was provided in a news story to show the path of an airliner before it crashed near Bolivia.

So, it comes down to this very abbreviated history: when there might have been the opportunity for Southport to develop a significant coaling operation, the ability to marshal sufficient interest and resources kept running into roadblocks. When that ability finally matured, the opportunity for a significant coaling operation had slipped away. Developments at Wilmington (dredging, warehouse and docks, stronger rail connections) supplanted Southport's potential viability. In its place, the railroad was relegated to small hauls generated by alternative industries and eventually succumbed to the much more efficient system of roads and highways in Brunswick County. To its enduring credit, however, the WB&S was instrumental in opening up the interior of Brunswick County, allowing for development of untapped resources and laying the groundwork for human settlement.

And this chapter now closes.

Epilogue

NEW BEGINNINGS

After World War II, the Department of the Army was tasked with developing a major supply depot. After considerable study, an area along the Cape Fear River about five miles upstream of Southport was formed into Military Ocean Terminal Sunny Point. Completed in 1955, this facility became the largest military terminal in the world. It required its own rail line, and a new one was built with the help of the Atlantic Coast Line Railroad, although it ran on a completely different path than the abandoned WB&S line.

Under the disciplined direction of the U.S. Army Corps of Engineers, the new rail line was established as a durable element of rail infrastructure. A railbed was properly built up, and fortified and heavy rails were mounted on strong crossties and ballasted with rock. In areas where the route crossed unstable terrain, a "land bridge" was built, essentially a trestle structure of driven pilings reinforced with packed earth and buried beneath topfill. Strategically placed culverts helped to alleviate effects of variable water pressure as the route traversed areas where currents flowed. The line is maintained in Class A condition by CSX Transportation.

In an unintended echo of the WB&S dedication nearly forty-five years earlier, special trains out of Wilmington carried dignitaries and celebrants to Sunny Point for speeches, salutes and other activities. Rail shipments now bring in all manner of military supplies and equipment, and the docks are capable of restocking enormous supply ships, which rotate on and off stations around the world for forward supply points.

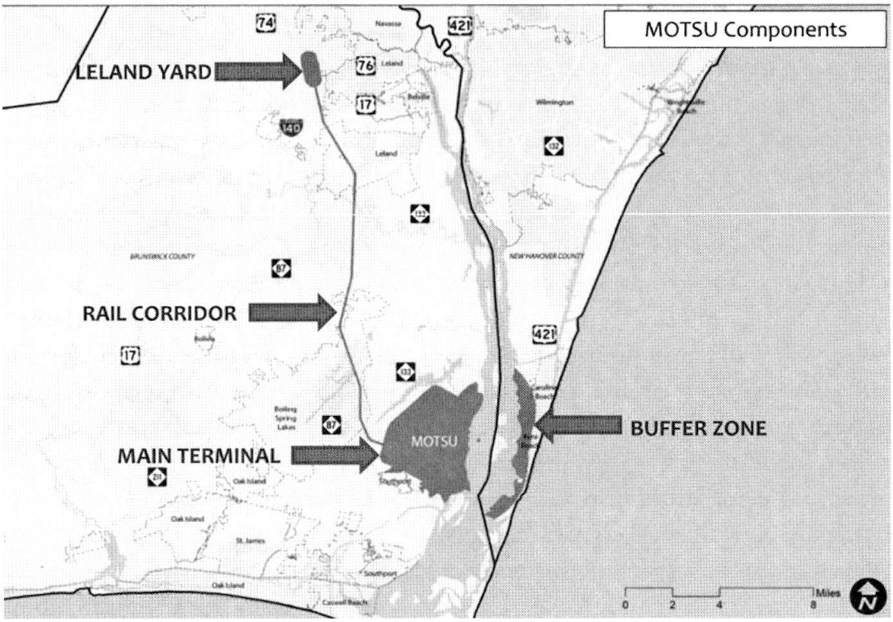

A map of the contemporary rail service to Sunny Point Military Ocean Terminal, developed in the 1950s to handle loading of military supply ships. Additional spurs (not shown) extend off the line toward Southport at the bottom. *"Military Ocean Terminal Sunny Point Joint Land Use Study," detail, Cape Fear Council of Governments, 2019.*

Additional spurs off this line provide rail access to Archer Daniels Midland, Capital Power and the Brunswick Nuclear Plant at the north edge of Southport.

In the early 1980s, when the fortunes of coal were once again ascendant (this time because of difficulties with oil supplies), a concept was briefly floated in Wilmington to transform about eighteen acres of riverfront land in the city to a coal export facility. Long supply trains, perhaps up to one hundred cars, would come in on CSX tracks to the riverfront, there to offload unnumbered tons of coal destined for overseas markets. The proposal was strongly opposed, however, with attention being called to the aesthetics of the existing character of downtown Wilmington and potential future designation for a convention center. In 1982, city voters approved a zoning amendment to ban coal terminals from areas designated as light industrial.

Southport retained its small-town character, as ever caressed by its "salubrious breezes" while its waterfront transitioned from a working character to one of scenic vistas and recreation. Unanticipated and

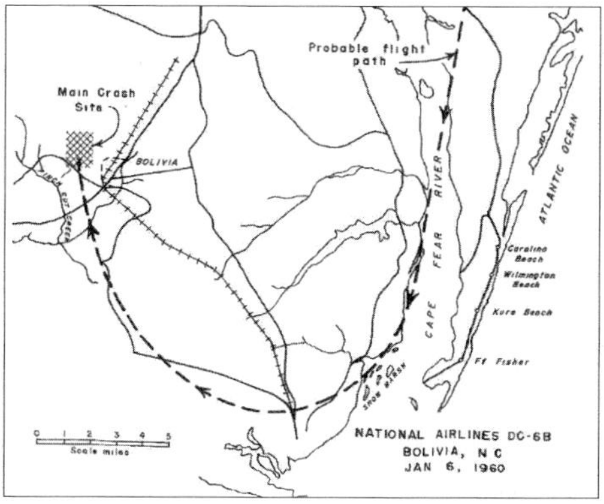

In 1960, National Airlines Flight 2511 crashed near Bolivia after taking off at Wilmington. The report on the accident included a map to show the plane's path. The long-abandoned route of the WB&S (crosshatched line) could still be used as a reference to help understand the area. *Civil Aeronautics Board Aircraft Accident Report, July 26, 1960.*

unwelcome "assistance" was provided by a couple of damaging hurricanes, notably Hurricane Hazel in 1954. Long gone are the quarantine station, coal dock, fish-processing plants and other shoreline structures. Still hemmed in by shore, marsh and woods, the town only grew slowly as residential and commercial developments were established outside its modest confines. Over the years, the sense of its history was captured and manifested in a maritime museum, museum of local history and preservation of historical landmarks and cultural sites.

Sometimes old ideas seem to be recycled. In 2006, a new idea was floated to develop major port facilities along the Cape Fear River upstream of Southport. Dubbed the North Carolina International Terminal, the concept was to re-channel the Cape Fear River, allowing a deep-water anchorage for large cargo ships along six hundred acres of land purchased by the North Carolina State Ports Authority. Some early enthusiastic commentary echoed certain portions of one-hundred-year-old sentiments about Southport's prominence on the Atlantic seaboard. Such developments were seen as a way to secure trade from the passage of larger ships nearly one thousand feet long and drafting almost forty feet. It was also obvious that such a facility would call for new rail connections to serve the volume of cargo that would be handled. Contentious from the outset, the project was eventually shelved.

In recent decades, there has been some popularity of repurposing old and vacated railroad rights-of-way for recreational uses. These rails-to-trails initiatives help to memorialize where the tracks ran while providing unique and often-scenic perspectives on the land through which they run. They also call for rehabilitation of the route, installation of appropriate safety measures, periodic maintenance and permission from landowners and civic jurisdictions. Perhaps most essential are beginning and end points that are

In a bit of a surprise, these rails were unearthed in about 2000 near East Brown Street and Rhett Street, right where the WB&S headed across the headwaters of Bonnet Creek in Southport. *Courtesy of Southport Historical Society.*

accessible to the public. In the case of the old WB&S route, the fragments that remain don't really go anywhere, and getting to them is a challenge. (At least we know where they are.)

Only time will tell if new iterations will surface, as they did in the many false starts leading to the organization of the Wilmington, Brunswick & Southern Railroad.

Appendix I

TRACING THE ROUTE OF THE WB&S

The railbed for the WB&S was never of very robust construction. Most often it was ballasted with compacted sand and clay drawn from alongside the path, with only the barest of embankment work. After all the rails and ties were removed in 1943, the path pretty much settled down to native grade. Some pieces became paved (or even unpaved) roads, while others became corridors for power transmission lines or were obliterated entirely during modern construction. Where traces remain, they can be described as follows, using contemporary place names and roadway designations. (For those interested in the wonky specifics, coordinates are also provided.) Starting from the north end, then:

Location	Coordinates
Diverge from CSX mainline north of Navassa (Navassa stop)	Path obliterated
Out Navassa Road (SR 1435) and across Sturgeon Creek	34.246, -78.001
At Old Fayetteville Road and WB&S Road	34.235, -78.006
Across Waterford and Magnolia Greens subdivisions	Path obliterated
Pick up on Dove Way, parallel to U.S. Highway 17 (Lanvale stop)	34.206, -78.052
Gradual convergent path to U.S. Highway 17 (El Paso stop)	Path obliterated

Location	Coordinates
El Paso was the name of a post office near what is now the Lanvale neighborhood. It existed fitfully from 1877 to 1909, although its place name would have carried on longer than that. For some years, it had a sawmill and turpentine still.	
Maco Road (NC Highway 87) crossing Bishop Branch	34.182, -78.085
Near bend along Zion Church Road, path crosses Town Creek Road or SR 1413 (Town Creek stop)	34.168, -78.094
Align with Cleveland Trail at Benson Road	34.161, -78.096
Green Hill Road (SR 1410) at Hollins Way, apparent old depot now destroyed, oriented parallel to old right-of-way (Winnabow stop)	34.148, -78.100
Brave Venture Drive at Bell Swamp Road (SR 1406)	34.116, -78.118
Along Corbett Street parallel to U.S. Highway 17 (Business) (Bolivia stop)	34.069, -78.152
Nearly right-angle bend to the southeast just south of Bolivia	34.063, -78.152
Path roughly parallel to Middle Swamp Creek, pick up at end of McKay Road (SR 1511)	34.055, -78.143
Along McKay Road across Green Lewis Road	34.047, -78.131
Ridge Road, intersection with West Boiling Spring Road (Laughlin?)	34.020, -78.081
Continue on Ridge Road tangent and parallel to unpaved "Craven Street"	34.011, -78.070
Extend tangent to cross unnamed road about 2,500 feet west of NC Highway 87 (Goresville?)	33.989, -78.049
Cross Long Beach Road (NC 133)	33.968, -78.036
Pick up path at end of Riedmount Street in Southport (Coolvale stop)	33.958, -78.036
Tangent across Dosher Cutoff, path obliterated	33.953, -78.030
Across Jabbertown Road (Atwood stop)	33.939, -78.025
Industrial spur branched off here to cross Dutchman's Creek to what is now a park	
Atlantic Avenue crossing East Leonard Street	33.924, -78.019
Slight bend to Rhett Street, along south edge of cemetery to Moore Street (Southport station)	33.921, -78.016

Alternatively, this is a list of modern place names, visual references and distance of places on the WB&S route where passengers or cargo could be handled. Some were just small basic country depots, open sporadically whenever there was activity to be conducted. Very early and impermanent waystops along the line also included Jackey's Creek, Loughlin, Goresville and Atwood.

Modern Place Name	**Modern Visual Reference**	**Miles from Navassa**	**Miles from Southport**	**Stops on WB&S 1929**
Navassa	Davis Yard (CSX)	0	30	Navassa*
Village Road and Navassa Road	Leland	2	28	Woodburn
Lanvale	Dove Way and Lanvale Road	6	24	Lanvale
Spring Hill	Hewett-Burton abd Goldman Roads at U.S. Highway 17	7	23	El Paso (obliterated by highway)
Town Creek	Town Creek Road near Zion Church Road	10	20	Town Creek
Winnabow	Green Hill Road west of U.S. Highway 17	11	19	Winnabow*
Winnabow	Bell Swamp Road and Brave Venture Drive	15	15	Brunswick Station
Bolivia	Corbett Street	17	13	Bolivia*
Boiling Spring Lakes	Ridge Road near 15th Road	20	10	Loughlin
Boiling Spring Lakes	Near Craven Street	23	7	Goresville
Coolvale	Crossing Dutchman Creek	28	2	Coolvale
Southport	West end of Jabbertown Road	28	2	Atwood
Southport	Rhett and Moore Streets	30	0	Southport*

* Had telephone service available

And for another alternative, these are close approximations of the major tangents (straight lines) surveyed along the route of the WB&S, using contemporary place names and reference points. Obviously, surveyors of the time had no access to GPS technology, so measurements and deflections can only be deduced by identifiable traces as seen in satellite photographic images—an exercise in "connecting the dots." With one exception, deflections are minor and noted by direction. A handy interactive overlay map can be found at *abandonedrails.com*. From the north end, then:

Tangent	**Distance**
Interchange with existing track in Navassa, down Navassa Road to Village Road (deflect north)	1.50 miles
Village Road to somewhere under interchange of U.S. Highway 17 and Interstate 140 (deflect south)	5.25 miles
Interchange of U.S. Highway 17 and Interstate 140 to near bend of Zion Church Road (deflect south)	1.50 miles
Near bend of Zion Church Road to Bell Swamp Road (deflect south)	3.50 miles
Bell Swamp Road to turn east at end of Corbett Street in Bolivia (nearly 90-degree turn east)	4.50 miles
Turn from Bolivia, down McKay Road, extended to deflection of Ridge Road (deflect south)	2.75 miles
Deflection of Ridge Road to Allen Creek (deflect south)	2.00 miles
Allen Creek to slight deflection 2,500 feet west of intersection Highway 133 and Highway 87 (deflect south)	3.00 miles
Deflection to Atlantic Avenue and East Eighth Street in Southport (deflect north)	3.75 miles
East Eighth Street and Atlantic Avenue to foot of Rhett Street in Southport	3,000 feet
SOUTHPORT STATION	

Appendix II

PLACES AND TRACES

Traces of the old WB&S route are all that remain today. Knowledge of its path can be inferred from place names along the route, and surface inspection helps stitch those places together on a map. High-resolution satellite photography identifies some stretches where the tracks ran, noted from slight changes in vegetation, especially when they run in straight lines. Finally, close-in map views from a service like Google Earth reveal property lines—with knowledge of the general path, the telltales are closely parallel lines, an indication of the old right-of-way. In some

Looking east, the WB&S route along Dove Way in Leland, near Lanvale Road. Extended across the current Magnolia Greens and Waterford developments, this would have connected to the end of WB&S Road off Old Fayetteville Road in Leland. *Photo by author, 2019.*

Left, top: Remnant of a freight depot in Winnabow (destroyed by a hurricane in 2018). Such informal locations along the route would hoist a signal if they wanted the train to stop there. *Photo by author, 2017.*

Left, middle: Looking east, McKay Road, running southeast from Bolivia. Where McKay Road ends, the tracks used to go straight ahead to what is now designated as Ridge Road along the southern edge of Boiling Spring Lakes. *Photo by author, 2019.*

Below: Emerging from wild growth from extending the tangent along McKay Road, this is where the path continues on to Ridge Road toward Allen Creek, south of Boiling Spring Lakes. *Photo by author, 2019.*

Left: Looking east, on the other side of Allen Creek, the path continues in more primitive form about parallel to the unfinished Craven Street south of Boiling Spring Lakes. Even after more than seventy-five years, the WB&S route still retains a semblance of endurance on its way to Southport. Barely twenty feet wide, this three-mile tangent is gradually reverting to native condition. *Photo by author, 2019.*

Below: A very stout bridge across a tendril of Orton Creek headwaters. Planks are six inches thick, and the distance between their centerlines is just under five feet, very nearly the distance needed to lay track at the standard gauge of four feet, eight and a half inches. Impressions in the remaining tar covering suggest a crosswise layer of additional timbers six inches wide and placed right next to each other. It is speculated that this is the only remnant of infrastructure along the WB&S. *Photo by author, 2019.*

places, the WB&S route itself is still indicated, although the roadbed lost any function decades ago.

Some portions of the route have been entirely effaced by land development, some portions have been paved to become named streets and roads, some portions have been repurposed as transmission corridors for electrical towers and portions have simply melted back into the landscape. Perhaps the most authentic remnant is the stretch of Ridge Road referenced at the beginning of this story—raised, composed of sand and clay, accompanied by a drainage ditch and running in a straight line for at least two miles.

Appendix III

WILMINGTON, BRUNSWICK & SOUTHERN RAILROAD POWER

The WB&S went through a variety of power units in its life. None of them were new, and getting information about any of them is sometimes an uncertain business. As best as can be determined, the collection included the following.

4-4-0 unknown American, wood fired: Most likely acquired with the purchase of property, structures and equipment of the R.W. Gibson sawmill and lumber operation at Town Creek. Of unknown make and provenance, it served the Town Creek Lumber and Railroad Company and then the WB&S with designation #100. It lasted until 1924, when it was traded in for another locomotive.

4-4-0 Rhode Island American, wood fired: Purchased by the WB&S in 1915 from Georgia Car and Locomotive. Designated #200, it saw service during the busy years of the company's life and in 1918 was sold to Southern Iron and Equipment Company.

There are hints of another locomotive in service around 1920, likely a 4-4-0 American, but nothing is known with certainty about this piece of equipment.

4-6-0 Baldwin #52661 ten-wheeler, oil fired: Designated #101, this was built in 1919 and originally saw service with Georgia Midland Railway. With a trade-in of #100, the WB&S acquired the locomotive in 1924, and it saw service for several years before being idled and eventually taken away no later than 1942 to be recycled for the war effort.

Brill GM68 motorcar or railcar: Given the designation of #11, this was a steel-body combine unit, fitted with a toilet compartment, seats for perhaps twenty or so passengers and a side freight door for small shipments of dry cargo and mail. After it was purchased by the WB&S in 1924, it was used until about 1933, when rail passenger service was discontinued. It gradually fell into derelict condition and would have been removed and scrapped no later than 1942.

Maintenance and inspection car: Of unknown vintage and make, a single grainy photo suggests an older touring sedan, modified to be able to run on the tracks.

0-6-0 Plymouth WL, diesel: This modest twenty-ton locomotive was built in 1928 and first saw industrial uses as a yard engine hauling coal and scrap metal. When the WB&S bought it in 1931 and designated it #600, it replaced the much heavier #101 for the declining number of freight shipments on a nonexistent schedule. After a few years, it, too, was relegated to retirement and would have been scrapped no later than 1942.

1934 Chevrolet "bus": This replaced the capabilities of the #11 motorcar, since rail passenger service had been discontinued. Built on a truck chassis, the "woody"-style body contained space for the mail, luggage and seats for about seven passengers.

1936 Chevrolet "bus": Built on a "stretch" truck chassis, this steel-body vehicle had a compartment for the mail and seating for perhaps eight to ten passengers. Definitely an upgrade from the earlier model it replaced.

Appendix IV

ASSOCIATED NAMES

The extraordinary number of attempts preceding the WB&S would naturally generate a lengthy list of associated principals and other interested parties. From a wide variety of sources, the following list was compiled of names related to railroad development out of Southport, employees and officers of the Wilmington, Brunswick & Southern Railroad and contemporaneous figures entering into the railroad's life. Generally, names are entered in chronological order by when they first appeared in news reports. Rarely, individuals may have reached prominent mention in later years.

Colonel David Risley: director, South Atlantic & Northwestern (1886, 1890)

J.B. Bilheimer: chief surveyor, South Atlantic & Northwestern (1886)

C.W. Staniford: chief engineer, South Atlantic & Northwestern (1887)

W.H. Phillips, R.J.S. Wood, L.F. Hepburn, Henry Belden, J.B. Bilheimer, J.F. Dane, W.R. Wilson, G.W. Edwards, Dr. W.G. Curtis: directors, South Atlantic & Northwestern (1888)

J.W. Coley: secretary, South Atlantic & Northwestern (1889)

Waldorf H. Phillips: president, South Atlantic & Northwestern (1887)

E.B. Stevens: of Chicago (Board of Trade); scout for South Atlantic & Northwestern (1889); moved to Smithville; advocate for Brunswick Western & Southern, Southern Terminal Railroad (1898); real estate agent to get riverfront property for WB&S (1912); enduringly involved in local affairs

John Wilson Brown: from Baltimore; president, Cape Fear & Cincinnati (1890)

George B. Morton: from Baltimore; general manager, Cape Fear & Cincinnati (1890)

J. Wilson Brown (president), George B. Morton (vice president), M.C. Guthrie (second vice president), J.H. Rowlenson (secretary), H.B. Ball (treasurer): officers, Cape Fear & Cincinnati

Dr. F.B. Ullery: vice president, Brunswick Western & Southern (1891)

John D. Bellamy: of Wilmington; attorney, Brunswick Western & Southern (1891); attorney, Carolina, Tennessee & Ohio (1896)

George H. Bliss: of Chicago; Brunswick Western & Southern (1891)

John C. Wiswell: of New York; president, Brunswick Western & Southern (1892)

S.L. Fremont: of Augusta, Georgia; owner of more than two hundred acres purchased by Brunswick Southern & Western (1892)

H.H. Dougherty: of New Jersey; general manager, Brunswick Southern & Western; incorporator, Southport Construction Company (1892); general superintendent, Carolina, Tennessee & Ohio (1896); officer, Southern Terminal Railroad (1898)

George L. Dunlop (president), F.B. Ulery (vice president), J.D. Bellamy (secretary/treasurer), George H. Bliss, R.W. Hicks, W.E. Worth, E.B. Stevens, W.H. Pike: directors, Brunswick Western & Southern (1892)

W.H. Pyke: of Southport; incorporator, Southport Construction Company (1892); director, Brunswick Western & Southern (1892); involvement with Carolina, Tennessee & Ohio (1896); railroad agent for Southport; real estate agent; insurance agent (1902)

William Weeks: of Southport; incorporator, Southport Construction Company (1892); builder (1902); died (1910)

J.C. Bayles: of New York; president, Cape Fear Harbor & Coal Company; to own Brunswick Southern & Western (1893)

W.A. Ray (president), John P. Neal (secretary), E.B. Stevens: officers, Southport & Western (1895)

Fremont, Costigan: families in Southport, property owners (1896)

Kate Stuart: of Southport, boardinghouse/hotel operator (1896), composes poem (1911)

Walter G. MacRae: of Wilmington; chief engineer, Carolina, Tennessee & Ohio (1896)

Frank H. Blodgett: of Ohio; general contractor, Carolina, Tennessee & Ohio (1896)

D.E. Blodgett: brother of general contractor Carolina, Tennessee & Western (1896)

J.D.L. Queen: Carolina, Tennessee & Ohio (1896)

J.A. Pullen: Carolina, Tennessee & Ohio (1896)

J.E. Challenger (president), Stephen Green (vice president), James Calhoun and P.R. Foley (secretary/treasurer), J.D. Bellamy, W.H. Pike, John R. Turrentine: directors, Carolina, Tennessee & Ohio (1892)

Thomas Bohannon: of Philadelphia; coal mine owner; operator for expected coal terminal by Carolina, Tennessee & Ohio (1896)

Carl Grubnau: of Philadelphia; wool merchant; backer of Carolina, Tennessee & Ohio (1896)

N.M. DeBruin (bridge timbers), R.P. Bodoin (foreman), Walter G. McRae (chief engineer), Henry McNeel (of Southport, chief cook), Louis London (commissary manger), George H. Bellamy (of El Paso, North Carolina, piling supplier), M. Fargussen (bridge engineer), J.T. Adams (ties): construction principals, Carolina, Tennessee & Ohio (1896)

W.W. Drew: of Southport, farmer where Indian evidence found (1896)

George H. Bellamy: of El Paso, North Carolina; piling supplier, Carolina, Tennessee & Ohio (1896); state senator; officer, Southport Terminal Railroad (1898); incorporator, WB&S (1907); director, WB&S (1911)

Judge McIver: receivership judge for Carolina, Tennessee & Ohio (1897)

John R. Turrentine Jr.: of Wilmington, purchaser of Carolina, Tennessee & Ohio assets (1897)

J.T. Adams: receiver, Carolina, Tennessee & Ohio (1897)

W.A. Cullen, Conrad Kirk, P. Murray, Henry McDougald, Thomas Hawkins, E.H. Cranmer, Frank Moer, C.C. Brown, A. Vorhees, H.H. Dougherty, George H. Bellamy, E.B. Stevens: directors and officers, Southport Terminal Railroad (1898)

W.A. Guthrie: of Durham; principal agent acting for Southport, Wilmington & Western (1899)

W.B. Guthrie: of Durham; principal for Southport, Wilmington & Western (1901)

Thomas L. Pray: of Durham; principal for Southport, Wilmington & Western (1901)

Charles N. Wire: of Philadelphia; principal shareholder, Southport, Wilmington & Western (1899)

James Warrington, John N. Reeve, J. Carpenter Rhoads, Johns C. Gessler, Charles C. Warwick, Horace G. Kimes: minority shareholders and directors, Southport, Wilmington & Western (1899)

Colonel Alfred F. Boone: of Zanesville, Ohio; reputedly planning coal hauling route from Tennessee to Southport (grander vision to establish link to Omaha, Nebraska) (1900)

John J. Knox: postmaster, El Paso, stop on WB&S (1902)

Alvin R. Morrison, William S. Hilles: president and secretary, Cape Fear Terminal Railroad (1902)

Horace G. Williams: contractor for Southport, Wilmington & Western (1903)

John Y. Gosler, Stephen Green, Chester E. Albright, Jesse B. Kime, D.W. Myers, F.L. Chestnut, John H. Chestnut, Frank C. Headman, E.H. Mangus, John C. Gosler: named defendants in action against Southport, Wilmington & Durham (1905)

John A. Mills: president, Raleigh & Southport (1905)

H.H. Dougherty, D.W. Bullock, W.J. Bellamy, George L. Morton, C.T. Bennett, J.H. Winston: shareholders, South Atlantic Terminal Co. (1905)

Martin McKinnon: of Red Springs; incorporator, Town Creek Lumber, second vice president for WB&S (1907)

J.H. Colvin: superintendent and construction manager, WB&S (1907)

S.A. Jones (president), B.J. Sloan (vice president), W.B. Williamson (treasurer), I.L. Councill (secretary), Alden Howell, F.R. Hewitt, W.B. Whitmire, Charles A. Wallen, R.A.L. Hyatt, M.D. Kingsland, D.L. Boyd, S.C. Welch, H.R. Ferguson, F.W. Miller, Thomas Stringfield, H.A. Love, John W. Norwood, Theodore F. Davidson, W.T. Weaver, S. Westray Battle, George L. Hackney: directors and officers, South Atlantic & Transcontinental (1907)

Colonel S.A. Jones: of Waynesville, North Carolina; mineral interests; organizer and proponent of the South Atlantic & Transcontinental (1908)

Charles W. Pearson: surveyor, South Atlantic & Transcontinental (1909)

Z.W. Whitehead: of Wilmington; incorporator (secretary/treasurer), Town Creek Lumber; president, WB&S (1907); drove last spike, dedicatory master of ceremonies (1911)

R.F. DeVane: of Red Springs; incorporator (president), Town Creek Lumber; secretary/treasurer, WB&S (1907)

A.J. McKinnon: of Maxton; incorporator (vice president), Town Creek Lumber; director, WB&S (1907)

Jackson Stanland: incorporator, WB&S (1907); Brunswick County sheriff, shot and killed (1908)

W.H. Chadbourn: incorporator, WB&S (1907)

C.J. Cooper: of Fayetteville; incorporator, Town Creek Lumber; first vice president, WB&S (1907)

R.W. McKeithan: incorporator, WB&S (1907); Bolivia agent; large lumber holdings

A.J. Fahneslock, J.E. Reason, Charles F. Belknap, F.S. Pusy, Thomas M. Stranger, A.P. Bauman: incorporators, Cape Fear, Southport & Atlantic (1907)

Thomas Ruffin Whitehead: son of Z.W.; drove first spike, WB&S (1907)

J.A. Mills: president, Raleigh & Southport (1909)

C.G. Remington: architect for Southport station (1911)

William Pinner: leader of Southport cheering group at dedication (1911)

John C. Mintz: of Wilmington; engineer (surveyor), WB&S (1907); greeter and escort at dedicatory event (1911)

Reverend K.B. Tupper: dedicatory invocation, WB&S (1911)

Robert W. Davis: attorney; welcome, dedicatory, WB&S (1911)

Joseph D. Smith: mayor, Wilmington; dedicatory remarks, WB&S (1911)

Hannibal L. Godwin: congressman; dedicatory speaker, WB&S (1911)

George Rountree: of Wilmington; attorney; dedicatory remarks, WB&S (1911)

Harry Skinner: of Greenville; attorney; dedicatory remarks, WB&S (1911)

J.O. Carr: of Wilmington; attorney; dedicatory remarks, WB&S (1911)

Lee S. Overman: of Salisbury; U.S. senator; dedicatory remarks, WB&S (1911)

F.M. Simmons: of New Bern; U.S. senator; dedicatory speaker, WB&S (1911)

W.W. Kitchin: governor; dedicatory speaker, WB&S (1911)

C. Ed. Taylor: dedicatory speaker, WB&S (1911)

Robert Ruark, J.B. Mercer, B. Dosher, J.H. Davis, Colonel Walker Taylor: of Southport, reunion organizers (1911)

Dr. Russell Bellamy: first passenger ticket, WB&S (1911)

F. Smith: engineer, WB&S (1911)

H.E. Goodwin: conductor, traffic manager, WB&S (1911)

~~~ Farrow: engineer, WB&S (1911)

J.D. Bateman: conductor, WB&S (1911)

John F. McNair: of Laurinburg; vice president, WB&S (1911)

Oscar Pearsall: of Wilmington; secretary-treasurer, WB&S (1911)

Martin McKinnon: of Red Springs; director, WB&S (1911)

Iredell W. McKeithan: of Lockwoods Folly; director, WB&S (1911)

Charles E. Taylor: director, WB&S (1911)

W.J. Tate: engineer, WB&S (1912)

W.E. Glenn: of Charlotte, contractor for WB&S terminal pier and wharf (1913)

G.J. Hart: clerk, WB&S (1914)

J.A. Springer: director, WB&S (1916)

F.B. Gault: director, WB&S (1916)

Eli Cavanaugh: Southport agent, WB&S (1919)

C.J. Field: of South Carolina; named traffic manager, WB&S (1920); retires (1923)

~~~ Grantham: engineer, WB&S (1920)

Charles E. Gause: Southport Fish Scrap Oil Co., before Wilmington commissioners (1922)

M.J. Corbett: president, WB&S (1921); appointed receiver (1933)

Charles Ruark: conductor, WB&S (1921)

Hubert M. Shannon: traffic manager; express agent, WB&S (1924); brought action for back pay (1933); organized Southport Railroad & Transportation Company (1941)

Roscoe Rogers: engineer, mechanic, WB&S (1920s)

Lottie May Newton: bookkeeper, WB&S (1920s)

Harvey Bryant: fireman, handyman, WB&S (1920s)

Homer Lanier: motorcar driver, WB&S (1924)

E. Cavenaugh: general agent, WB&S (1926)

J.W. Brooks: vice president, WB&S (1926)

Mac McGlamery: worker at CCC Camp Sapona (circa 1934)

Rollie Walton: driver, WB&S "bus" (circa 1935)

Percy Canady: part-time engineer, WB&S (1930s)

William H. Walker, Martin Marlow: injured in station explosion (1940)

A.N. Manucy, R.C. MacNeal, E.F. Middleton, P.O. Mead, H.B. Smith, S.B. Frink, Hubert Shannon: incorporators, Southport Railroad & Transportation Co. (1941)

~~~ Cumbee: driver, WB&S Lines (1942)

Hubert Livingston: general manager, WB&S Bus Lines (1945)

Maurice Goodman: owner, WB&S Bus Lines (1948)

William Walker, Herman Phelps, Ralph Phelps, W.H. Stephenson: drivers, WB&S Bus Lines (1949)

SOURCES

Organized archives were of great help and, in a digitized online world, far easier and more economical to explore than spending endless hours finding and delving into hard-copy material. Some of the online resources included the Southport Historical Society and its Susie Carson Research Room, a repository of images, narratives, names and much more about that town. Especially useful in the early going was *Chronology of Southport* by Bill Reaves, a five-volume compilation of historical notes and news items covering four hundred years of development. Southport's local newspaper, the *State Port Pilot*, provided valuable visual memories in the collected photographs of the "The Way It Was" series. The North Carolina Digital Collection at the University of North Carolina at Chapel Hill also provided much in the way of digitized historical archives, particularly in its maps, newspaper and city archives. Finally, the digitized compilations found at newspapers.com (a division of Ancestry), ncpedia.org (North Carolina Government and Heritage Library at the State Library of North Carolina) and digitalnc.org offered a wide-ranging survey of information and many newspapers across North Carolina and around the country. Naturally, with newspapers as image sources, graininess is a given, what with the methods of printing at the time.

American Rails. www.american-rails.com. Online compendium of all things railroad: history, companies, manufacturers, Amtrak, contemporary railroads, museums, etc.

Botkin, B.A., and Alvin F. Harlow, eds. *A Treasury of Railroad Folklore*. Bonanza Books, 1953.

Coleman, Alan. *Railroads of North Carolina*. Charleston, SC: Arcadia Publishing, 2008.

Curtis, Margaret Coit. Personal diary, 1886–96, Southport Historical Society (2008).

DeGolyer Library, Southern Methodist University.

Google Maps. Internet accessible, these continually updated maps can be magnified or reduced and moved to examine different areas. Of much value is the feature of temporal compilation, whereby obscure historical place names or surface attributes continue to be included, allowing discoveries of locations for long-gone settlements and communities, lot line or extinct railroad routes.

Kennedy, George A. "Wilmington, Brunswick, and Southern Railroad." 2006. www.ncpedia.org.

Kernan, Charles. *Rails to Weeds: Searching Out the Ghost Railroads around Wilmington*. N.p., 1988.

Landmark Preservation Associates. *Comprehensive Historical/Architectural Site Survey of Brunswick County, North Carolina*. 2010.

Lee, Lawrence. *The History of Brunswick County, North Carolina*. Brunswick County, NC: Heritage Press, 1980. Extensively researched overview of two hundred years of development; especially useful for placing events in context of surrounding circumstances.

Lewis, J.D. carolana.com.

North Carolina Corporation Commission. *Annual/Biennial Reports*. E.M. Uzzell State Printers, 1907–34.

North Carolina Government and Heritage Library. ncpedia.org.

North Carolina Newspaper Collection, State Archives of North Carolina.

Nunn, Scott. "Locals Share Memories of Rail Line between Wilmington, Southport." StarNewsOnline.com, July 24, 2012.

Official Guide of the Railways. N.p., 1929, 1934, 1937.

Ozog, Edward J. "Rhode Island Locomotive Works," https://sites.google.com/site/rhode islandlocomotiveworks/

Pratt, Joseph Hyde. "Good Roads Movement in the South." *Annals of the American Academy of Political and Social Science* (January 1910).

Reaves, Bill. *Chronology of Southport.* Extensive compilation of news items and features (attributions to primary sources mostly absent). Southport Historical Society, Susie Carson Research Room, Southport, NC.

———. *The Lake Counties: Yesterdays.* Newspaper series, 1973–75.

Register of Deeds, Brunswick County, North Carolina, 1905–07.

Reports of the Department of Labor, North Carolina. www.digital.ncdcr.gov.

Southport Historical Society, PO Box 10014, Southport, NC 28461.

"Southport Oral History Interviews." University of North Carolina–Wilmington Archives and Special Collections, 1995.

Strouse, L.K. *Decisions of the Interstate Commerce Commission of the United States.* Interstate Commerce Commission, Vol. 125, 1927.

Thirteenth Census of the United States. U.S. Department of Commerce, 1910.

———. Bulletin, Occupation Statistics: U.S. Department of Commerce Bureau of the Census, 1910.

United States Geological Survey maps. Exceptionally detailed, these provide valuable insights over time about roads, highways, geological features, waterways, structures, railroad routes and much more. Section maps reviewed included Southport (1946), Funston (1943), Winnabow (1943), Wilmington (1943), Bolivia (1943).

Wikipedia. "WikiProject: Trains." en.wikipedia.org/wiki/Wikipedia:WikiProject_Trains.

Wilmington, North Carolina Directory, 1911–1912. N.p.: Hill Directory Company, 1912.

Wilmington, North Carolina Directory, 1919. N.p.: Hill Directory Company, 1919.

The online digital compilations of newspapers.com and digitalnc.org provided access to many publications, and searches for relevant terms yielded results from these publications. Given a network of telegraphic dispatches, identical stories could be found in quite a few newspapers, only sometimes attributed to a source publication.

Alamance Gleaner
Asheville Gazette-News
Asheville Weekly Citizen
Atlanta Constitution
Brunswick Beacon (Shallotte, NC)
Carolina Watchman (Salisbury, NC)
Charlotte Evening Chronicle
Charlotte News
Charlotte Observer
Democratic Banner (Mount Vernon, OH)
French Broad Hustler (Hendersonville, NC)
Gastonian Gazette
Goldsboro Headlight
Greensboro Patriot
Grit (Siler City, NC)
Lenoir Topic
Monroe Journal
New Bern Weekly Journal
Polk County News
Raleigh Evening Visitor

Raleigh Farmer & Mechanic
Raleigh News & Observer
Robesonian (Lumberton, NC)
Southport Leader
Southport Standard
Spartanburg Herald
State Port Pilot (Southport, NC)
Statesville Record and Landmark
Western Sentinel (Winston-Salem, NC)
Wilmington Daily Review
Wilmington Dispatch
Wilmington Journal
Wilmington Messenger
Wilmington Morning Star
Wilmington Post

Interviews: John Kopp (Bolivia), Frank Galloway (Bolivia), Alex McKay (Waynesville)

Reviewer acknowledgements: Jim Kapetsky, Marilyn Raschka, Bob Surridge, Calverna Koenig

ABOUT THE AUTHOR

Mark Koenig was born and raised in Milwaukee, Wisconsin.

Armed with bachelor's and master's degrees in business, he worked for eighteen years in healthcare management, developing strategic plans, analyses of activity, marketing and business development initiatives and special projects. These activities provided the understanding that current events are rarely linear. Instead, they require a broader awareness that many factors influence the way forward and must be considered.

A redirection in career led to management of a community orchestra, where administrative activity had to be coordinated with artistic disciplines. Besides marketing and planning, thought had to be given to the creation of enjoyable concert experiences across seasons of performances.

A move to Wilmington, North Carolina, yielded the opportunity to direct the Wilmington Railroad Museum, just in time to oversee its relocation and launch a new era in interpreting and presenting the story of railroad history and heritage. Here were the seeds of this first book, where the story of a local short line could be examined at length, weaving together various threads of history, old recollections, geography, economic forces and insights about personalities. Following retirement after twelve years with the museum, work could begin in earnest on this work.

He and his wife live in Leland, North Carolina.